2-18-75

Sartre: a study

Sartre: a study

by
BRIAN MASTERS

HEINEMANN
London
ROWMAN AND LITTLEFIELD
Totowa, New Jersey

ISBN 0 435 37581 4 (Heinemann)
ISBN 0 87471 496 6 (Rowman and Littlefield)

© Brian Masters 1970
First published in the Students' Guide to European
Literature series 1970
Reprinted 1972
First published in this edition 1974

Published in Great Britain by
Heinemann Educational Books Ltd
48 Charles Street, London W1X 8AH
This edition published in the United States
by Rowman and Littlefield, Totowa, New Jersey
Printed in Great Britain by
Fletcher & Son Ltd
Norwich

Contents

Foreword — ix

Acknowledgements — xi

Biographical Note — xiii

Chapter One: LA CONTINGENCE — 1

Chapter Two: FROM ABSURDITY TO FREEDOM — 9

Chapter Three: LA MAUVAISE FOI,
or THE REFUSAL OF FREEDOM — 19

Chapter Four: CHOICE AND RESPONSIBILITY — 38

Chapter Five: ACTION — 44

Chapter Six: L'ENGAGEMENT — 56

Chapter Seven: CONCLUSIONS — 66

Chapter Eight: THEORY — 72

Bibliography — 81

to Trevor

Foreword

In common with the general policy of the Student Guides Series, this book is intended as a preliminary introduction to more detailed study. The books of Jean-Paul Sartre are important to students of literature, philosophy, and political theory; the present author has chosen to concentrate on the first aspect of his work. No attempt has been made to discuss Sartre's political analyses, and only the briefest sketch of his ontological theory is offered in the final chapter to illustrate its relation to his fictional works. This book is intended primarily for the student of French literature, and it makes considerable use of quotations from a large body of Sartre's work to allow, as far as possible, Sartre to be his own interpreter.

Wherever possible, page references to quotations given in the text relate to the cheapest available editions, on the assumption that these will be the most readily accessible to the student. Quotations from the following books all refer to editions in the Gallimard *Livre de Poche* series:

> *La Nausée*
> *Le Mur*
> *Les Chemins de la Liberté*
> I. *L'Age de Raison*
> II. *Le Sursis*
> III. *La Mort dans l'Ame*

Page references to quotations from *Baudelaire* and *Qu'est-ce que la Littérature?* refer to the editions in Gallimard's *Collection Idées*.

Quotations from other works (*L'Être et le Néant, L'Existentialisme est un Humanisme, Saint Genet, Situations I, Situations II, Les Mots*) are taken from the original editions, to be found in a more complete bibliography on page 81. No page references are given for quotations taken from plays, of which there are a variety of inexpensive editions.

All quotations are given in the original French.

B.M.
Wynyard, 1969

Acknowledgements

The author wishes to thank the following publishers for permission to quote passages from the works of Jean-Paul Sartre of which they control the copyright:

LIBRAIRIE GALLIMARD (*La Nausée, Le Mur, Les Mouches, L'Être et le Néant, L'Age de Raison, Le Sursis, La Mort dans L'Ame, Huis-Clos, Baudelaire, Les Mains Sales, Situations I & II, Le Diable et le Bon Dieu, Saint-Genet, Les Mots*).

EDITIONS NAGEL (*L'Existentialisme est un Humanisme*).

Thanks are also due to EDITIONS DU SEUIL for permission to quote from *Sartre par lui-même* by Francis Jeanson, to the UNIVERSITY OF MICHIGAN PRESS for a passage from *Jean-Paul Sartre* by Norman N. Greene, and to POLYDOR RECORDS LTD. for the passage taken from Sartre's introduction to their recording of *Huis-Clos*.

The author wishes to thank in addition Mr Maurice Cranston for permission to quote from his book *Sartre*, and M. Jean-Paul Sartre for his agreement to include passages from his many works.

Gratitude is expressed to Mr E. K. Timings for his careful reading of the manuscript, and to A. L. for affording the incomparable tranquillity of his home at Wynyard in which to write this book.

Biographical Note

Jean-Paul Sartre was born in Paris on 21 June 1905. His father died two years later, and he was brought up in the household of his maternal grandfather, Karl Schweitzer, a strict authoritarian and Puritan. His mother remarried when Jean-Paul was eleven years old.

He was educated at the Lycée Henri IV in Paris, and then at the École Normale Supérieure, from which he graduated in 1929. There followed National Service, and then almost six years as teacher of philosophy at the lycée in Le Havre; this period was interrupted only by a year spent in Berlin, where Sartre studied the German philosophers.

Just before the war, he taught at the Lycée Pasteur in Neuilly. His first book was a philosophical essay, *L'Imagination*, published in 1936. But it was not until 1938 that he became famous, with the publication of *La Nausée* and *Le Mur*. Sartre was captured and imprisoned by the Germans soon after the war broke out, but was released on the grounds of poor health after a few months (he wrote a play for the prisoners during these months called *Bariona*). Upon his return to Paris, and until the end of the war, Sartre played an active and influential part in the French Resistance movement. He also resumed teaching and writing. His greatest philosophical work, *L'Être et le Néant*, appeared in 1943, and in the same year his play *Les Mouches* was performed in Paris.

At the close of war, Sartre abandoned his teaching career in order to devote himself entirely to writing. He founded a political and literary revue, *Les Temps Modernes*, produced a number of plays and continues to write on a wide variety of political and social themes.

Sartre now lives in Paris, in close association with a fellow writer and philosopher whom he met at the École Normale when he was still a student, Simone de Beauvoir.

1

La Contingence

The starting-point for an understanding of Jean-Paul Sartre's vision of the human condition is an examination of the important concept of 'la contingence'; this is best achieved by reading his first novel, *La Nausée* (1938), which contains the germ of his later philosophical work.

La Nausée is the diary of one Antoine Roquentin, a highly introspective intellectual living in the provincial town of Bouville, where he is engaged in writing a biography of the Marquis de Rollebon.

The diary explores a crisis in Roquentin's philosophical development, namely his discovery of the nature of existence, and the pain and terror which this discovery causes him. In philosophical terms, Roquentin discards the comfortable and reassuring doctrine of Essentialism in favour of a profoundly disquieting Existentialist view of the physical world. In personal terms, this discovery results in the anguished realization that nothing in the world carries any inherent meaning or value.

To follow the course of this discovery and its effect upon Roquentin, we must first understand what is meant by the terms *Essentialism* and *Existentialism*.

A. Essentialism and Existentialism
The *essence* of an object is the sum of the properties which are particular to that object and which distinguish it from any other. Thus the essence of a circumference is that it is composed of the joining of points which are all situated equidistant from another point called the centre.

An *Essentialist* view of the world maintains that everything which exists is defined by its essence, which it carries within itself and which cannot be applied to anything else. The empirical world, as well as the mathematical world, makes excellent sense in this case, since any object is explicable in terms of its exclusive definition; there is no mystery. Put in another way, essence precedes existence; the immutable and inescapable definition of an object occurs in logical sequence before that object exists, and will apply *whether or not* the object exists.

Roquentin admits that, like everyone else, he too had assumed that everything had an inherent meaning, composed of a list of its qualities. He had never before questioned the meaning of existence, he says, but had taken it for granted:

1. Je pensais *l'appartenance,* je me disais que la mer appartenait à la classe des objets verts ou que le vert faisait partie des qualités de la mer. Même quand je regardais les choses, j'étais à cent lieues de songer qu'elles existaient: elles m'apparaissaient comme un décor.

   (La Nausée, pp. 179–80)

But, in the throes of his crisis, while gazing at the root of a chestnut-tree, Roquentin is made to realize that this complacent view of the world was grotesquely erroneous:

2. le monde des explications et des raisons n'est pas celui de l'existence. Un cercle n'est pas absurde, il s'explique très bien par la rotation d'un segment de droite autour d'une de ses extrémités. Mais aussi un cercle n'existe pas. Cette racine, au contraire, existait dans la mesure où je ne pouvais pas l'expliquer . . . la fonction n'expliquait rien: elle permettait de comprendre en gros ce que c'était qu'une racine, mais pas du tout *celle-ci* . . . (elle) était au-dessous de toute explication.

   (Ibid, p. 183)

The kernel of this discovery is that *Existence precedes Essence,* that things exist without explanation or reason.

A man-made utilitarian object, such as a hammer, clearly does possess an essence, which was present in the artisan's mind before the hammer was made. But Roquentin is more concerned with things which exist completely independently of man's presence or will.

Also, a mathematical abstraction may be defined by its essence, but since a mathematical abstraction does not exist, it is irrelevant.

The abstract idea of 'a root' may also contain an essence and be defined by it *a priori*, but such a definition does not explain why this particular root *exists* in its physical, tangible presence.

Existence is a brute fact, unrelated to abstract ideas. Existentialism is concerned with concrete reality, and not with mental exercises. Thus the list of properties which define the concept 'root' are unacceptable, because they do not explain why this particular root *is there*.

Roquentin suffers an emotional reaction to this discovery, conveyed in his attitude to and relation with the *Things* which surround him.

B. Les Choses

In contact with inert matter, Roquentin experiences a certain physical disgust with the viscosity of *Things* and with their impudent lack of justification. He almost feels that, baldly existing without reason, they are insulting. Furthermore, their profusion and ineluctability inspire him with a fear bordering on panic:

1. J'appuie ma main sur la banquette, mais je la retire précipitamment: ça existe . . . je suis au milieu des Choses, les innommables. Seul, sans mots, sans défenses, elles m'environnent, sous moi, derrière moi, au-dessus de moi. Elles n'exigent rien, elles ne s'imposent pas: elles sont là.

   (Ibid, p. 177)

2. Je ne pouvais plus supporter que les choses fussent si

proches . . . je suffoque: l'existence me pénètre de partout, par les yeux, par le nez, par la bouche.   (Ibid, p. 178)

3. des masses monstrueuses et molles, en désordre – nues, d'une effrayante et obscène nudité.   (Ibid, p. 180)

4. Tous ces objets . . . comment dire? Ils m'incommodaient.
(Ibid, p. 180)

Hence, *la nausée* in the first place refers to the feelings of distasteful repugnance, 'cette espèce d'écoeurement douceâtre' (p. 22), which Roquentin experiences in the presence of Things. Maurice Cranston has called this a 'religious sensibility which shrinks from the physical world and perceives it as entirely viscous'.

C. De Trop

·Having once discovered that the material world is meaningless, it is only one step further for Roquentin to become shatteringly aware that his own existence is equally absurd. He feels 'de trop', unnecessary, unjustified in a world of unjustifiable objects, 'in the way', obscene and vulgar; what is he *doing there*? He feels that he is just as unwarranted and ludicrously senseless as the *Things* whose impudent emptiness he has just intuited:

1. Je n'avais pas le droit d'exister. J'étais apparu par hasard, j'existais comme une pierre, une plante, un microbe.
(Ibid, p. 122)

2. Et moi, – veule, alangui, obscène, digérant, ballottant de mornes pensées – *moi aussi j'étais de trop*.
(Ibid, p. 181)

The knowledge that he is 'de trop' sets Roquentin apart from his fellows, who feel that he is different and cannot understand him:

3. Tout d'un coup, j'ai perdu mon apparence d'homme, et ils ont vu un crabe qui s'échappait à reculons de cette salle si humaine.   (Ibid, p. 175)

The sensation of being 'de trop' in the world is a characteristic common to many of Sartre's heroes, though they are not all lucid enough to perceive the cause of the sensation. Hugo, in the play *Les Mains Sales* (1948), confesses:

> 4. Je suis de trop, je n'ai pas ma place, et je gêne tout le monde.

In his essay on *Baudelaire* (1947), Sartre expounds the idea that the poet's anguish stemmed from a similar feeling of being 'de trop', without his knowing precisely why. And Mathieu Delarue, the central character of the trilogy *Les Chemins de la Liberté*, feels that he is as ugly and unwarranted a protuberance as a pile of refuse:

> 5. Il était de trop: une grosse immondice au pied du mur.
> (*L'Age de Raison*, p. 105)

In his autobiographical essay *Les Mots* (1963), Sartre reveals that he himself, as an infant, already suffered from such disorientation:

> 6. Je découvrais tout à coup que je comptais pour du beurre et j'avais honte de ma présence insolite dans ce monde en ordre.
> (*Les Mots*, p. 70)

> 7. Respirant, digérant, déféquant avec nonchalance, je vivais parce que j'avais commencé de vivre.
> (Ibid, p. 71)

D. La Contingence

Having acknowledged the fearful truth that neither the Things which surround him (the boulevard, the root of the chestnut-tree, etc.), nor he himself are in any way *necessary*, Sartre concludes (and Roquentin *is* Sartre, as he tells us in *Les Mots*) that the nature of existence lies in the fact that it is both *gratuitous* and *contingent*. The dictionary gives one definition of 'contingent' as 'chance or accidental'. 'J'étais apparu par hasard', says Roquentin in the quotation given above. Things exist without any reasonable justification, without any pre-established 'essence', without any absolute necessity for existing. They simply 'are'. We see now that 'la nausée' is rather more than a physical repulsion from contact with Things; it is an affective repugnance progressing to a seizure of intellectual terror at the valueless, worthless character of existence, which Roquentin elsewhere calls, with undisguised loathing and anger, 'cette ignoble marmelade', and which plunges him into 'une extase horrible'.

1. L'essentiel, c'est la contingence. Je veux dire que, par définition, l'existence n'est pas la nécessité. Exister, c'est *être là*, simplement; les existants apparaissent, se laissent *rencontrer*, mais on ne peut jamais les *déduire* . . . Tout est gratuit, ce jardin, cette ville, et moi-même . . . Voilà la Nausée.   (*La Nausée*, p. 185)

2. Tout existant naît sans raison, se prolonge par faiblesse, et meurt par rencontre.   (Ibid, p. 188–9)

3. l'existence – qui n'est jamais bornée que par l'existence . . . cette profusion d'êtres sans origine.
(Ibid, p. 187)

4. le monde tout nu qui se montrait tout d'un coup, et j'étouffais de colère contre ce gros être absurde . . . bien sûr il n'y avait *aucune raison* pour qu'elle existât, cette larve coulante. *Mais il n'était pas possible* qu'elle n'existât pas.   (Ibid, p. 190)

Existence is an incomprehensible proliferation of Beings, none of which have any reason for 'being there'. As absurdly unjustified as inanimate matter, Man is thrown into the world without choice, devoid of purpose. He has no 'essence' to bolster him up, which would define him in advance and lend a reason to his existence; he simply 'is'. And yet, however much his existence may lack design or purpose, he cannot cease to be. He is there, utterly naked and vulnerable against a backcloth of absurdity, amid a profusion of unjustifiable and worrying entities, with no recourse to theories or systems which might justify his being there in the first place.

Sartre later makes a very clear and precise distinction between the two verbs 'to be' and 'to exist'. Being is a description of a passive state; it requires no will, no effort, no reason, to 'be'. The root of the chestnut-tree *is*, and Roquentin feels that he himself *is*; hence his anguish and solitude. In order to *exist*, a resolute effort of lucidity and consciousness is required, as we shall see later; man can transcend his state of being and achieve a process of existing. Things can not.

To summarize: The *Essentialist* finds the world of Being easily comprehensible in terms of *a priori* definitions. These definitions, or *essences*, are arrived at by a process of cold, theoretic deduction, and are expressed in terms of abstract concepts. The definition of an object thus precedes the existence of that object.

The *Existentialist* finds the world of Being incomprehensible and gratuitous. Abstract concepts can only explain abstractions, he says, and have nothing to do with reality. Existence is a bald, grotesque, ugly, disconcerting but inescapable fact, beyond the realm of definitions or explanations. It is concerned with concrete reality, for which the existence of an object precedes the definition, or possible definitions, of that object. Furthermore, this truth is *felt* rather than thought out, it starts from an intuition which manifests itself in physical terms, and produces a kind of *nausea*. (Sartre frequently expresses his disgust with the gratuity of existence by laying heavy emphasis on those bodily functions which are the most unpleasant, such as digestion, defecation, etc.)

Lastly, the revelation of the *Contingence* of existence makes Sartrean man in turn *frightened, agonized, disgusted*, and deeply *angry*.

We must now see the ways in which the fundamental absurdity of all existence is manifested, and especially what it entails. Once it is accepted that both material existence and human life are devoid of reason or sense, where does man go from there? Does he merely flounder in a despairing morass of negativity, or can he draw any positive conclusions from his discovery? Sartre's answer is that the emptiness of the world makes the lucid man who perceives it, first desperately *alone*, and then utterly *free*. . . . .

2

From Absurdity To Freedom

A. Absurdity

1. Le mot d'Absurdité naît à présent sous ma plume.
    (La Nausée, p. 182)

The startling revelation that everything which exists has no reason for existing sparks a response within Roquentin which can only be described as a sudden awareness that the world is founded upon a terrible but unyielding absurdity. This is not so much an idea which he works out, as a reaction to his experience with Things.

2. Je comprenais que j'avais trouvé la clé de l'Existence, la clé de mes Nausées, de ma propre vie. De fait, tout ce que j'ai pu saisir ensuite se ramène à cette absurdité fondamentale.
    (Ibid, p. 182)

Not only is this Absurdity all-pervading and unshakeable, it is also cruelly inescapable; there is no arguing with it, no denying it, no issue from it. It may be beyond the realm of Reason, but it traps even reasonable beings:

3. *Ils n'avaient pas envie* d'exister, seulement ils ne pouvaient pas s'en empêcher; voilà.
    (Ibid, p. 188)

Absurdity also manifests itself, in a less dramatic way, to Lucien, the central character in *L'Enfance d'un Chef*, one of five short stories published under the collective title *Le Mur* in 1939:

4. *Rien* n'a *jamais* aucune importance.   *(Le Mur, p. 183)*

Lucien experiences the feeling that his existence is gratuitous,

that he has no control over it or part in it, and that it would not
matter very much if he did not exist at all:

5. Lucien ne savait que faire de son corps; quoi qu'il entre-
   prît, il avait toujours l'impression que ce corps était en
   train d'exister de tous les côtés à la fois, sans lui demander
   son avis.   (Ibid, p. 171)

6. – Qui suis-je? Je regarde le bureau, je regarde le cahier.
   Je m'appelle Lucien Fleurier mais ça n'est qu'un nom.
   Je me gobe. Je ne me gobe pas. Je ne sais pas, ça n'a pas
   de sens ...' ... Lucien frissonna et ses mains trem-
   blaient: Ça y est, pensa-t-il, ça y est! J'en étais sûr: *je
   n'existe pas.*   (Ibid, p. 172)

Roquentin is an intellectual, Lucien a schoolboy. The latter's
experience of Absurdity is therefore less lucidly expressed. But
both experiences are emotional rather than mental, and both
are provoked by a contemplation of Things. Lucien considers
his desk, the blackboard, his exercise-book, his body, and *then*
himself.

Mathieu, the main character in *Les Chemins de la Liberté*, a
projected series of four novels of which three have so far been
published, is similarly aware of the fundamental lack of
importance attached to what he is and what he does. Mathieu is
in fact the most perfect embodiment of the ineffective intellectual who views the absurdity of life and shrugs his shoulders.
He is apathetic, disinterested, unconcerned. He contrives to
remain anonymous, 'n'importe qui', and does not consider
that the senselessness of human existence is any of his business.
Bored, he washes his hands of the problem and yawns. For the
length of the first two volumes of *Les Chemins de la Liberté*
his attitude in face of the absurdity of the world is one of
langorous amusement, and refusal to have any opinion:

7. Cette vie lui était donnée pour rien, il n'était rien et
   cependant il ne changerait plus; il était fait . . . Il bâilla.
                              (*L'Age de Raison*, p. 441)

Absurdity reveals itself to Baudelaire, in Sartre's psycho-
analytic study, as a function of his *uselessness*. The poet suffers
because, knowing that his existence is unjustified, he can see no
way of investing it with any purpose:

> 8. Or elle (la conscience) se saisit d'abord dans son entière
>   gratuité, sans cause et sans but, incréée, injustifiable,
>   n'ayant d'autre titre à l'existence que ce seul fait qu'elle
>   existe déjà. Elle ne saurait trouver hors d'elle des pré-
>   textes, des excuses ou des raisons d'être, puisque rien ne
>   peut exister pour elle si d'abord elle n'en prend conscience,
>   puisque rien n'a d'autre sens que celui qu'elle veut bien y
>   attacher. De là l'intuition si profonde chez Baudelaire de
>   son inutilité.   (*Baudelaire,* p. 34)

If nothing can excuse, explain or justify a purposeless and
motiveless existence, man is thereby plunged into a profoundly
solitary anguish.

B. L'Angoisse

> 1. Nous sommes angoisse   (*L'Être et le Néant,* p. 81)

Deprived of an established system of meanings and motives
with which to explain the world, man is alone and unprotected.
Sartre's work is full of references to man's emptiness, bewilder-
ment, and puzzlement in face of the Absurd. In some cases,
this loneliness is expressed as *an exile* from the logical world, a
feeling-apart, an outsider, as for example with Mathieu in *Le
Sursis*:

> 2. Je ne suis rien, je n'ai rien. Aussi inséparable du monde que
>   la lumière et pourtant exilé, comme la lumière, glissant à
>   la surface des pierres et de l'eau, sans que rien, jamais, ne
>   m'accroche ou ne m'ensable. Dehors. Dehors. Hors du
>   monde, hors du passé, hors de moi-même.
>   (*Le Sursis,* p. 419)

Oreste, in *Les Mouches* (1943), feels his loneliness as a kind of
leprosy:

    3. seul comme un lépreux.

    4. je me suis senti tout seul, au milieu de ton petit monde
       bénin, comme quelqu'un qui a perdu son ombre.

While Baudelaire gives expression to his profound isolation in
many poems which have as their theme the vertiginous plung-
ing of man into a bottomless abyss:

    5. il se voit jusqu'au fond du coeur, incomparable, incom-
       municable, incréé, absurde, inutile, délaissé dans l'isole-
       ment le plus total, supportant seul son propre fardeau ...
       replié dans la contemplation, et en même temps, jeté hors
       de lui en une infinie poursuite, un *gouffre* sans fond, sans
       parois et sans obscurité.   (*Baudelaire,* p. 49)

There is a danger that the lucid man who perceives Absurdity
and the isolation into which this perception casts him might
enjoy a paradoxical sense of security at having solved the
enigma of the world and might pursue the experience no
further, as if *angoisse* and *inquiétude* were sufficient ends in
themselves. The danger is particularly acute in the case of the
intellectual, as for example Roquentin in *La Nausée*, or
Mathieu in *Les Chemins de la Liberté*. Such indulgence Sartre
has himself confessed to in *Les Mots*, referring to the period
when he wrote *La Nausée*:

    6. Dogmatique, je doutais de tout sauf d'être l'élu du doute;
       je rétablissais d'une main ce que je détruisais de l'autre et
       je tenais l'inquiétude pour la garantie de ma sécurité;
       j'étais heureux.   (*Les Mots,* p. 210)

This kind of intellectual arrogance leads nowhere. *Angoisse* is a
purely negative result of the knowledge of the Absurd. There
is a more positive and useful outcome, which is the awareness
and acceptance of *Freedom*.

C. La Liberté

Thus far, we have seen that reality is contingent, gratuitous and
absurd, both in its application to man and to the multifarious

objects which surround him. Neither he nor they have any essence which justifies their existence.

But the first breakthrough in this depressing vision of the world comes when man realizes that he is the only reality which can *change*; the power of consciousness or awareness invests him with the ability to create his own essence *a posteriori*, whereas thoughtless, inanimate matter is fixed for ever in its absurd state. Essence may precede Existence as far as abstract concepts are concerned, but man does not have to live with abstractions, he must live with reality, so abstract values are worthless to him. In the world of reality, Existence precedes Essence. He therefore exists first, and subsequently creates his own essence, which Things cannot do. Things are trapped, imprisoned in a mire of non-meaning. Man is free, free from pre-conceived definitions, free from pre-ordained values. He is free to define himself and to create his own values. The knowledge of this freedom which lifts him above the world of Things comes as a blinding revelation:

1. Je suis libre, Électre (says Oreste in *Les Mouches*), la liberté a fondu sur moi comme la foudre.

Once man has acknowledged this all-important liberty which distinguishes human reality from the rest of reality, he must cast aside all abstract notions of *Good* and *Evil*. Such values no longer exist in a determined state. They are movable values, which are relative to each given situation and are impossible to define in advance in a rigid code. Every man is free to create his own Good and Evil, at every moment of his life. He is suddenly released from the shackles of dogmatic morals and inflexible absolutes. And once he is aware of this freedom, there is no turning back, and there is no power which can deprive him of it:

2. Quand une fois la liberté a explosé dans une âme d'homme, les Dieux ne peuvent plus rien contre cet homme-là ...

C'est aux autres hommes – à eux seuls – qu'il appartient
de la laisser courir ou de l'étrangler.

(Jupiter in *Les Mouches*)

It is for this reason that Oreste refuses to repent his crime,
denies even that it is a crime. The murder which he has committed was right at that time and in that situation. He kills
Egisthe and his mother, Clytemnestra, not to avenge his father,
as Electre wanted him to, for such would be to accept the value
of the abstract idea of 'vengeance'. He kills Egisthe to free the
people of Argos from tyranny, and as he does so, he says:

3. Que m'importe Jupiter? La justice est une affaire d'hommes, et je n'ai pas besoin d'un Dieu pour me l'enseigner.

So saying, he creates his own 'justice' and invents his own
essence, or justification for existing. This act is therefore 'good'
in the Sartrean sense, since it is the expression of a sudden
eruption of freedom. It is only 'bad' if one accepts that Good
and Evil are permanent, unshakeable realities. They are not,
and so the murder is no crime at all:

4. J'ai fait mon acte . . . et cet acte était bon . . . Je ne suis
pas un coupable, et tu ne saurais me faire expier ce que
je ne reconnais pas pour un crime . . . . . . il n'y a plus rien
eu au ciel, ni Bien, ni Mal, ni personne pour me donner
des ordres.

Mathieu, also, in *La Mort dans l'Ame*, finally experiences a
similar moment of freedom, which he no longer rejects with his
customary apathy, freedom to act according to the situation
and not according to precedent. He is trapped in a village church
with three friends during the war, when the Germans arrive,
and he knows that there is no hope. Instead of surrendering,
they open fire on their enemy, and all are killed save Mathieu.
He then continues to shoot wildly, and with each shot he
destroys one imprisoning Abstract Idea after another:

5. Il tirait, les lois volaient en l'air, tu aimeras ton prochain
comme toi-même, pan dans cette gueule de con, tu ne

tueras point, pan sur le faux jeton d'en face. Il tirait sur
l'homme, sur la Vertu, sur le Monde: la Liberté, c'est la
Terreur ... il tira sur le bel officier, sur toute la Beauté
de la Terre, sur la rue, sur les fleurs, sur les jardins, sur
tout ce qu'il avait aimé. La Beauté fit un plongeon obscène
et Mathieu tira encore. Il tira: il était pur, il était tout-
puissant, il était libre.

(*La Mort dans l'Ame*, pp. 280–1)

Again, Baudelaire, according to Sartre, has a moment of
lucidity during which his fundamental Freedom is revealed:

6. Pour avoir choisi la lucidité, pour avoir découvert malgré
   lui la gratuité, le délaissement, la liberté redoutable de la
   conscience, Baudelaire s'est placé devant une alternative;
   puisqu'il n'est pas de principes tout faits auxquels
   s'accrocher, ou bien il lui faudra stagner dans un in-
   différentisme amoral ou bien il inventera lui-même le
   Bien et le Mal.   (*Baudelaire,* p. 50)

We shall see in a subsequent chapter, however, that Baudelaire
in a curious way refuses to accept this terrifying freedom and
continues to bow to the abstract notions of Good and Evil.

It is for the reasons stated above that Sartre reproaches
François Mauriac, in a famous article reproduced in *Situations
I,* for refusing to allow his characters to be free. Mauriac's
characters, says Sartre, are fabricated in advance, their essences are fixed; whatever action they take is therefore predict-
able, and determined by their nature:

7. Si je soupçonne que les actions futures de héros soient
   fixées à l'avance par l'hérédité, les influences sociales ou
   quelque autre mécanisme, mon temps reflue sur moi. ...
   Voulez-vous que vos personnages vivent? Faites qu'ils
   soient libres.   (*Situations I*, p. 37)

And, in the same volume of *Situations*, Sartre devotes an essay
to the consideration of Cartesian liberty, which he finds a
negative liberty, since Descartes allows God alone to be the
creator of Good and Evil. This essay I shall also examine more
closely in its proper place.

Sartrean freedom, though absolute, does contain an element of restriction. It is a terrifying freedom, because there is no release from it. One is *obliged* to invent values at every minute. We are free to interpret anything at any time, free to construct values on impulse, free to give sense to a senseless world, but we are continually and constantly *obliged* to exercise this freedom. We cannot abdicate. We have not chosen to exist, we have not chosen to be free, but we *do* exist and we *are* free, and we are therefore constrained perpetually to use this freedom, whether we like it or not. This is the meaning behind one of Sartre's most frequently quoted sentences, which comes from *Le Sursis*: 'je suis condamné à être libre.' (p. 419). And Oreste says much the same thing in *Les Mouches*: 'je suis condamné à n'avoir d'autre loi que la mienne ... Car je suis un homme, Jupiter, et chaque homme doit inventer son chemin.'

In a lecture which was subsequently published under the title *L'Existentialisme est un Humanisme* in 1946, Sartre explains the significance of his understanding of freedom in this way:

8. L'Existentialiste ... pense qu'il est très gênant que Dieu n'existe pas, car avec lui disparaît toute possibilité de trouver des valeurs dans un ciel intelligible; il ne peut plus y avoir de bien *a priori*, puisqu'il n'y a pas de conscience infinie et parfaite pour le penser; il n'est écrit nulle part que le bien existe, qu'il faut être honnête, qu'il ne faut pas mentir, puisque précisément nous sommes sur un plan où il y a seulement des hommes. Dostoïewsky avait écrit: 'Si Dieu n'existait pas, tout serait permis'. C'est là le point de départ de l'Existentialisme. En effet, tout est permis si Dieu n'existe pas, et par conséquent l'homme est délaissé, parce qu'il ne trouve ni en lui, ni hors de lui une possibilité de s'accrocher. Il ne trouve d'abord pas d'excuses. Si, en effet, l'existence précède l'essence, on ne pourra jamais expliquer par une référence à une nature humaine donnée et figée; autrement dit, il n'y a pas de déterminisme, l'homme est libre, l'homme est liberté .... Nous sommes seuls, sans excuses. C'est ce que j'exprimerai

en disant que l'homme est condamné à être libre. Condamné, parce qu'il ne s'est pas créé lui-même, et par
ailleurs libre, parce qu'une fois jeté dans le monde, il est
responsable de tout ce qu'il fait.

(*L'Existentialisme est un Humanisme,* pp. 35-7)

Critics are generally unanimous in dismissing this brief essay
as contradictory and superficial; Sartre has himself expressed
dissatisfaction with it. But the careful student will nevertheless
find it useful in so far as it summarizes the fundamental
subjectivity of all existentialist ontologies, and throws some
light on Sartre's own view of the characters who appear in his
novels and plays.

(*a*) An intuition of *contingence* has led to a refusal to rely on
theoretic *essences* to explain the meaning of existence, and a
correlative acceptance that existence must therefore be meaningless and *absurd*.

(*b*) Man is thus *free*, in his *solitude*, to attach whatever meanings he wishes to existing things, including himself, free to
create his own *significances*.

(*c*) But this freedom is not optional, there is no escaping it.
By his very condition as the only being that can invent essences,
he is *obliged to be free*, and constantly to exercise this freedom.
Whatever he does, he will be creating *meanings*:

9. L'Homme existe d'abord, se rencontre, surgit dans le
   monde, et se définit après.   (Ibid, p. 21)

Freedom is thereby stated as a *fact*, not as a value. There is no
arguing with the fact that man is free. It is by exercising this
freedom that he creates values. By facing up to it and embracing
it, he is able to make of it a valuable power.

The vast majority of men, however, spend their lives in a
frantic flight from freedom. Unable to face the solitude and
anguish which we have seen are affective results of an awareness of freedom, they attempt to avoid it in various ways, and
to construct a protective security for themselves which will
absolve them from the awful necessity of being free.

Sartre reserves his most hostile contempt for those who alienate their freedom, either by running away from it, or by misusing it. His message is that such an attempt is doomed to failure anyway, since freedom is inalienable.

In the following chapter I shall consider some of the great museum of types which people the pages of Sartre's novels and plays, all of whom are running away from freedom or abusing it.

3

La Mauvaise Foi
or The Refusal of Freedom

Sartre demonstrates the full meaning of existentialist Freedom by, in the first instance, showing how men seek to deny it or avoid it. Afraid of the yawning emptiness which Freedom implies, they try at all costs to *pretend* that they are *not* free, that they are not abandoned and alone in a meaningless world:

1. Certes, beaucoup de gens ne sont pas anxieux; mais nous prétendons qu'ils se masquent leur angoisse, qu'ils la fuient ... on n'échappe à cette pensée inquiétante que par une sorte de mauvaise foi.
   (*L'Existentialisme est un Humanisme* pp, 28–9)

Mauvaise foi involves culpability. In Sartrean morality, the worst criminal is he who, through fear, attempts to mask his freedom, elude the personal effort which must be required to give a meaning to the world, and make of himself as fixed and rigidly determined an entity as the immutable things which surround him. By denying that he is free, he evades the unpleasant responsibility of having to *do* anything; he can remain safe in the belief that he is what he is because he has always been so. He has his rightful place in a world which is meaningful and sensible; he can merely 'be', as a thing 'is', passively; he can only obey the rules. Baudelaire is guilty of just such *mauvaise foi*:

2. Peut-être on *n'est* pas pour soi-même à la manière d'une chose. Peut-être même on *n'est* pas du tout: toujours en

c

question, toujours en sursis, peut-être doit-on per-
pétuellement *se faire.* Tout l'effort de Baudelaire va être
pour se masquer ces pensées déplaisantes. ... Il est
l'homme qui, éprouvant le plus profondément sa condition
d'homme, a le plus passionément cherché à se la masquer.
(*Baudelaire,* pp. 49–50)

3. Il a comme une intuition profonde de cette contingence
   amorphe et obstinée qu'est la vie.... il en a horreur parce
   qu'elle reflète à ses yeux la gratuité de sa propre conscience,
   qu'il veut se dissimuler à tout prix.   (Ibid, p. 131)

This is why Baudelaire writes so many poems about the beauty
of the city, where he feels secure and justified:

4. il n'a plus *sa* place nulle part, il est posé sur la terre, sans
   but, sans raison d'être comme une bruyère ou une touffe
   de genêt. Au milieu des villes, au contraire, entouré
   d'objets précis dont l'existence est déterminée par leur
   rôle, et qui sont tous auréolés d'une valeur ou d'un prix, il
   se rassure: ils lui renvoient le reflet de ce qu'il souhaite
   être: une réalité *justifiée.*   (Ibid, p. 133)

Supposing that a man should decide that he *wants* to deny his
freedom, that he *wants* to take refuge in *mauvaise foi*; shouldn't
he be free to do so? Sartre's answer is that of course he should,
but in so doing he is committing an error. Having acknowledged liberty, says Sartre in *L'Existentialisme est un Humanisme,* a strictly coherent attitude must be to use it, not to
hide it. And Sartre defines those who *do* hide it as either
'cowards' or 'swine':

5. je puis former des jugements sur ceux qui visent à se
   cacher la totale gratuité de leur existence, et sa totale
   liberté. Les uns qui se cacheront, par l'esprit de sérieux
   ou par des excuses déterministes, leur liberté totale, je les
   appellerai lâches; les autres qui essaieront de montrer que
   leur existence était nécessaire, alors qu'elle est la contingence même de l'apparence de l'homme sur la terre, je les
   appellerai des salauds.
   (*L'Existentialisme est un Humanisme,* pp. 84–5)

The *lâches* (cowards) find all manner of pretences to avoid facing up to their freedom, the *salauds* (swine) establish a rigid code of immutable values, and seek to enforce obedience to this code on to their fellow-men.

Mauvaise foi adopts many methods to achieve a flight from reality:

A. Les Comédies Humaines

By attaching importance to the banality of everyday life, what Heidegger[1] has called *Alltäglichkeit*. All actions then have the emptiness of gestures. Those who choose this method are acting a part, leading an *inauthentic* life.

B. Le Passé

By living according to the past, identifying oneself with what one was and has always been, and refusing to progress or advance.

C. L'Autrui

By living according to the image others have made of one, and fulfilling their expectations.

D. Les Salauds

By claiming their 'rights' and just deserts according to a system of ready-made values, established by others.

E. Easy Answers

By pretending to give meaning to existence in theoretic systems, such as Humanism or Aestheticism.

[1] *Martin Heidegger*. Born in 1889, Heidegger became Professor of Philosophy at Freiburg in Breisgau, after having taken, and renounced, holy orders. His greatest work is *Being and Time*.

A. Les Comédies Humaines

In *La Nausée*, Roquentin observes with contempt the ludicrously self-important daily routines of the bourgeois inhabitants of Bouville (which is the fictitious name for Le Havre), and concludes that such ceaseless immersion in banality is a way to avoid recognition of the Absurd:

1. il faudra qu'ils trouvent autre chose pour voiler l'énorme absurdité de leur existence. Tout de même ... est-il absolument nécessaire de se mentir?
    Je parcours la salle des yeux. C'est une farce! Tous ces gens sont assis avec des airs sérieux, ils mangent. Non, ils ne mangent pas: ils réparent leurs forces pour mener à bien la tâche qui leur incombe. Ils ont chacun leur petite entêtement personnel qui les empêche de s'apercevoir qu'ils existent; il n'en est pas un qui ne se croie indispensable à quelqu'un ou à quelquechose.

    (La Nausée, p. 158)

Thus, by reducing their lives to a succession of mechanical gestures, they can absolve themselves from thinking and, perhaps, reaching painful conclusions.

The work of Sartre is full of instances of such people. In his principal philosophic treatise, *L'Être et le Néant*, he gives the example of the café waiter who fulfils his trivial tasks with an air of importance:

2. Considérons ce garçon de café. Il a le geste vif et appuyé, un peu trop précis, un peu trop rapide, il vient vers les consommations d'un pas un peu trop vif, il s'incline avec un peu trop d'empressement, ses yeux expriment un intérêt un peu trop plein de sollicitude pour la commande du client. ... Il joue, il s'amuse. Mais à quoi joue-t-il? Il ne faut pas l'observer longtemps pour s'en rendre compte: il joue à *être garçon de café.*

    (L'Être et le Néant, pp. 98–99)

An almost identical example occurs in *Les Chemins de la Liberté.* It is Mathieu who makes the observation:

3. Il était un peu trop barman, il secouait le shaker, l'ouvrait,

faisait couler une mousse jaune dans des verres avec des gestes d'une précision légèrement superflue: il jouait au barman. (*L'Age de Raison*, p. 254)

The intensity of such empty routine gestures makes both the barman and waiter mere actors who are playing a part, fulfilling a role assigned to them. Their lives are thereby robbed of *authenticity*.

Hugo, in *Les Mains Sales,* is aware of the inauthentic character of his life. None of his emotions are genuine, they are assumed:

3. Vous croyez peut-être que je suis désespéré? Pas du tout: je joue la comédie du désespoir.

Even his love-making with his wife Jessica is inauthentic. They are both playing at being in love, and each one in addition is pretending to believe that the other is in love.

Similarly, Goetz, in the play *Le Diable et le Bon Dieu*, admits that his life has been a pretence:

4. Tout n'était que mensonge et comédie. Je n'ai pas agi! J'ai fait des gestes.

One does not have to look far to find manifold examples of such ostrich-type self-satisfaction in everyday life, and one must allow that it is frequently unconscious, although Sartre would regard this as an 'excuse' and a consequence of 'cowardice'. Lucien's parents are seen dragging out their petty lives in cretinous bliss, much like a couple of Ionesco characters:

5. Papa et Maman jouaient à être Papa et Maman; maman jouait à se tourmenter parce que son petit bijou mangeait si peu, papa jouait à lire le journal et à agiter, de temps en temps, son doigt devant la figure de Lucien en disant: 'Badaboum, bonhomme!' Et Lucien jouait aussi mais il finit par ne plus très bien savoir à quoi. A l'orphelin? Ou à être Lucien? ... Lucien eut soudain l'impression que la carafe jouait aussi à être une carafe. ... Il pensa qu'il en avait assez de jouer à être Lucien. Il ne pouvait

pourtant s'en empêcher et il lui semblait tout le temps qu'il jouait.

(L'Enfance d'un Chef, in *Le Mur,* pp. 157–8)*

Even the young Sartre himself, as he tells us in *Les Mots,* felt that he was an impostor-child:

> 6. J'étais un faux enfant, je tenais un faux panier à salade; je sentais mes actes se changer en gestes. La Comédie me dérobait le monde et les hommes; je ne voyais que des rôles et des accessoires.   *(Les Mots,* p. 67)*

The writer Jean Genet, to whom Sartre has devoted an exhaustive and fascinating study which tells us as much about Sartre as it does about Genet, was forced into an inauthentic life by the demands of others, who placed labels on him. His larceny, his pederasty, his revolt against authority and against norms, were the signs of a reluctant playing out of a role which had been cast for him. Genet provides the most complete example of the way in which one lives a life according to the demands of others, as we shall see below.

Hugo, Goetz, Lucien, young Sartre, Genet, even Oreste before he commits the act which recognizes his Freedom, are all in the end 'actors', whose roles are assigned, unreal, ungenuine. The epitome of such a type is of course the professional actor, and it is significant that Sartre should choose to write a play about the famous English actor Kean (after Alexandre Dumas). Kean is never quite sure when he is acting and when he is not; his two personae become fused into one impostor:

> 7. Est-ce que je sais, moi, quand je joue? Est-ce qu'il y a un moment où je cesse de jouer? Regardez-moi: est-ce que je hais les femmes ou est-ce que je joue à les haïr? Est-ce que je joue à vous faire peur et à vous dégoûter, ou est-ce que j'ai très réellement et très méchamment envie de vous faire payer pour les autres?   *(Kean)*

Each and every one of these characters, from the bourgeois

of Bouville to Kean the actor, have an attitude in common: a sometimes wilful, sometimes lazy desire to opt out of the authentic life; a culpable wish to bury themselves in routine, meaningless gestures, instead of facing up to their Freedom and accepting the challenge which it offers. As Roquentin says, they live their lives 'comme s'il la racontait. Mais il faut choisir, vivre ou raconter.' (*La Nausée*, p. 60)

B. Le Passé

Another way in which one can cover up one's Freedom is to lose one's identity in the past, in one's own past; to continue being the person one thinks one has always been, and continue assuming the values one has always assumed. It would therefore be useless to be free, since freedom cannot change me, or the world! It is again Roquentin who is given the most eloquent exposé of this vice:

1. Ils vivent au milieu des legs, des cadeaux, et chacun de leurs meubles est un souvenir. Pendulettes, médailles, portraits, coquillages, presse-papiers, paravents, châles. Ils ont des armoires pleines de bouteilles, d'étoffes, de vieux vêtements, de journaux; ils ont tout gardé. Le passé, c'est un luxe de propriétaire.

   (*La Nausée*, p. 96)

2. Commode passé! Passé de poche, petit livre doré plein de belles maximes. 'Croyez-moi, je vous parle d'expérience, tout ce que je sais, je le tiens de la vie.' Est-ce que la Vie se serait chargée de penser pour eux? Ils expliquent le neuf par l'ancien – et l'ancien, ils l'ont expliqué par des évènements plus anciens encore, comme ces historiens qui font de Lénine un Robespierre russe et de Robespierre un Cromwell français: au bout du compte, ils n'ont jamais rien compris du tout. ... Derrière leur importance, on devine une paresse morose: ils voient défiler des apparences, ils bâillent, ils pensent qu'il n'y a rien de nouveau sous les cieux.   (Ibid, p. 101)

Likewise, though in a more pathetic way, Baudelaire turns his

back not only on the future, but on the present. His past self is
the only identity he can be sure of:

> 3. il a choisi d'avancer à reculons, tourné vers le passé,
>   accroupi au fond de la voiture qui l'emporte et fixant son
>   regard sur la route qui fuit. Peu d'existences plus stag-
>   nantes que la sienne. Pour lui, à vingt-cinq ans, les jeux
>   sont faits.   (*Baudelaire*, p. 206)

Baudelaire expresses his chase after the past by means of the
masochistic remorse in which a great body of his poems indulge. Remorse and regret are symptomatic of a backward-
looking thought, which releases one from the obligation of
inventing new and fresh meanings for one's life. Baudelairian
remorse is, in Sartre's eyes, an easy way out: the memory of
what he was satisfies his furious desire to have an 'essence', and
he only then commits evil in order to repent it, and thereby
confirm this essence:

> 4. Vivre c'est tomber; le présent est une chute; c'est par le
>   remords et le regret que Baudelaire a choisi de ressentir ses
>   liens avec le passé. . . . il se retourne vers ce passé qu'il *est*
>   et qu'il croit avoir souillé; il réalise une appropriation à
>   distance de son essence et, du même coup, il retrouve la
>   joie perverse de la faute. Mais cette fois ce n'est pas contre
>   la vertu enseignée qu'il prêche: c'est contre lui-même. Et
>   plus il s'enlise dans le mal, plus il se donne d'occasions de
>   se repentir, plus vivant et plus pressant devient le souvenir
>   de ce qu'il a été, plus solide et plus manifeste le lien qui
>   l'unit à son essence.   (*Baudelaire*, pp. 218–19)

That Baudelaire should define himself as 'he who suffers
continual remorse for the Evil which he wilfully commits' and
feel safe in the protection of this 'essence' indicates that he has
refused the Freedom which would allow him to invent his own
Good and Evil in each new situation. One can only regret that
which one feels to be 'wrong' in a world of permanent values.
Baudelaire commits evil not as an expression of his Freedom,
but, paradoxically, as a denial of it, because he accepts the pre-

ordained definition of Evil. The truly free person, in the Sartrean sense, cannot possibly show remorse for past acts, since each act is *ipso facto* 'good' as long as it springs from an awareness of freedom from the eternal concepts of Good and Evil. This is why Oreste, in the passage quoted earlier, refuses to repent his crime of murder on the grounds that Good and Evil do not exist, and the act cannot therefore be stigmatized as a crime. For Baudelaire, on the contrary, Good and Evil do exist in eternity, and he is for ever punishing himself for committing evil. Hence his retrospective fascination with his own past.

C. L'Autrui

He who makes a wilful effort to 'be' the person others see in him and to consciously play the role they have cast for him, is also alienating his freedom. Whereas those like the barman and the waiter 'play' at life because they are largely unaware that they have any alternative, Baudelaire, for example, has admitted his freedom but abnegates it by making himself a willing prisoner of the image which he sees reflected in the eyes of others:

1. Mais qu'est-ce au fond que Satan sinon le symbole des enfants désobéissants et boudeurs qui demandent au regard paternel de les figer dans leur essence singulière et qui font le mal dans le cadre du bien pour affirmer leur singularité et la faire consacrer? (*Baudelaire,* p. 124)

2. un souci extraordinaire et constant de l'opinion. Il se sait vu, il sent perpétuellement les regards sur lui; il veut plaire et déplaire à la fois; le moindre geste est 'pour le public'. (*Baudelaire,* pp. 193–4)

3. Il se voit ou tente de se voir comme s'il était un autre. (Ibid, p. 105)

It is also partly for the same reason that Baudelaire has made himself into a famous dandy; he finds some measure of security in the image of a dandy, but it is a false and unreal image.

Lucien in *L'Enfance d'un Chef* has seized the gratuitous nature of his existence very early in life, together with his resultant freedom. But the effort of using it is too great for him, and he decides instead to fit the mould of an image already created by others:

> 4. Le vrai Lucien – il le savait à présent – il fallait le chercher dans les yeux des autres, dans l'obéissance craintive de Pierrette et de Guigard . . . Tant de gens l'attendaient, au port d'armes: et lui il était, il serait toujours cette immense attente des autres. (*Le Mur*, p. 243)

At the very end of the story, Lucien makes up his mind that he will after all have a right to live if he becomes, as everybody expects, a leader of men, 'un chef'. His life will no longer be absurd, for he will have rights and duties which will give it a purpose. In Sartrean terms, however, this decision is cowardly, since it is not born of a will to use Freedom, but of a desire to become a social object which exists only in an artificial order manufactured by others. *L'Enfance d'un Chef* is in fact a study of an embryo Fascist.

The play *Huis-Clos* shows very clearly how much a coward requires other people to sustain the illusion he has of himself. Three characters are trapped for eternity in Hell together. One of them, Garcin, is a coward in the Sartrean sense, but tries to persuade himself that he is not a coward by constructing an image of himself as a strong man in the eyes of another character, Estelle. This image is patently a lie, and Estelle refuses to confirm it:

> 5. GARCIN: Estelle, est-ce que je suis un lâche?
> ESTELLE: Mais je n'en sais rien, mon amour, je ne suis pas dans ta peau. C'est à toi de décider.

In the same play, the third character, Inès, says to Estelle:

6. Viens! Tu seras ce que tu voudras: eau vive, eau sale, tu te
   retrouveras au fond de mes yeux telle que tu te désires.

Since all three characters are dead, they really do not have
Sartrean freedom at all. They can never become anything
other than they are, and are condemned to throw back at one
another images of each other to sustain them. There is no
escape, no possibility of freedom to create their own meanings.
This is the real significance of the oft-quoted phrase taken from
this play: 'L'Enfer, C'est les autres'.

In the course of his spoken introduction to the recording
of *Huis-Clos*, Sartre says:

7. c'est une mort vivante que d'être entouré par le souci
   perpétuel de jugements et d'actions que l'on ne veut pas
   changer... J'ai voulu montrer par l'absurde l'importance,
   pour nous, de la liberté, c'est-à-dire l'importance de
   changer les actes par d'autres actes. Quel que soit le
   cercle d'enfer dans lequel nous vivons, je pense que nous
   sommes libres de le briser. Et si les gens ne le brisent pas,
   c'est encore librement qu'ils y restent. De sorte qu'ils se
   mettent librement en enfer.

Perhaps the best example of a man transfixed in the petrifying
gaze of the Other is Daniel in *Le Sursis*, since he, in all consciousness, prefers the living death to which Garcin, Estelle
and Inès are condemned. Daniel, a homosexual obsessed
with guilt, seeks the sleep and peace of complete lethargy,
which he can best achieve by seeing himself as the object as
others see him:

8. Être de pierre, immobile, insensible, pas un geste, pas un
   bruit, aveugle et sourd... une statue farouche aux yeux
   blancs, sans un projet, sans un souci.... Être ce que je
   suis, être un pédéraste, un méchant, un lâche, être enfin
   cette immondice qui n'arrive même pas à exister... Être
   pédéraste comme le chêne est chêne. S'éteindre. Éteindre
   le regard intérieur... Être comme ils me voient.

   (*Le Sursis*, p. 155)

But, naturally enough, Daniel finds that, dependent as he is on the presence of others to assure him that he *is* something, his security is transient, ephemeral; he ceases to *be* as soon as he is alone:

> 9. J'ai toujours tout fait pour un témoin. Sans témoin, on s'évapore ... Je suis las d'être cette évaporation sans répit vers le ciel vide, je veux un toit.   (Ibid, p. 228)

The only *permanent* gaze to which Daniel can aspire is the gaze of God; he therefore finally takes refuge in religion. Bathed in the constant love of God, he eventually finds peace, calm, tranquillity; he need no longer question, interrogate himself, make himself. He is, for ever, as the other sees him, a homosexual with a capital H. In a letter to Mathieu, Daniel writes:

> 10. Je sais enfin que je suis. Je transforme à mon usage et pour ta plus grande indignation, le mot imbécile et criminel de votre prophète, ce 'je pense donc je suis' qui m'a tant fait souffrir – car plus je pensais, moins il me semblait être – et je dis: on me voit, donc je suis. Je n'ai plus à supporter la responsabilité de mon écoulement pâteux: celui qui me voit et me fait être; je suis comme il me voit ... je dis à Dieu: me voilà. Me voilà tel que vous me voyez, tel que je suis. Qu'y puis-je? vous me connaissez et je ne me connais pas. Qu'ai-je à faire sinon à me supporter? Et vous, dont le regard me suit éternellement, supportez-moi. Mathieu, quelle joie. ... Je suis infini et infiniment coupable. Mais je suis, Mathieu, je suis. Devant Dieu et devant les hommes, je suis. *Ecce homo*.   (Ibid, pp. 469–70)

We have considered:

(*a*) Those who play the comedy of banal everyday life because they are blind to their fundamental freedom, such as Kean, the bourgeois of Bouville, the barman, the waiter;

(*b*) those who have experienced the revelation of freedom, but escape from it into the past (Baudelaire, more bourgeois in Bouville);

(c) those who sink themselves into a personality they see reflected in the eyes of The Other (Baudelaire again, Garcin, Lucien).

All three types are *des lâches* in Sartrean terminology. They all are petrified into fixed, immutable *objects*, as gluey, viscous and repulsive as the *Things* which surround them. Afraid of the chasm which *Freedom* opens up before them, they either turn away from it or reject it, and fall into a stagnant state of simply 'being there'. No effort to invent meaning is then required. A dream to reduce oneself to the level of a Thing, to objectivize oneself ('être de pierre, immobile, insensible . . . sans un projet, sans un souci')*, is what constitutes 'la lâcheté'.

11. Son souhait le plus cher est d'*être*, comme la pierre, la statue, dans le repos tranquille de l'immuabilité.
(*Baudelaire*, p. 215)

The dead characters of *Huis-Clos* present a special case since, by virtue of their death, they are unable to interpret, or contribute to the meaning of their own existence; they are objectivized into the state of a Thing, for ever.

D. Les Salauds

Worse than the 'lâches' are the 'Salauds', who force others to conform to their own petrification.

– the *lâches* deny their own freedom
– the *salauds* seek to rob others of their freedom

Basking in a false tranquillity, blithely sure of themselves, refusing to question or doubt that their existence is justified, the *salauds* strive to impose their own ancient system of handed-down values on their fellow-men. They claim Right and Reason for their own, thus making everyone who does not conform to their order feel guilt and inadequacy:

1. Ces types qui ne doutent jamais de rien ni d'eux-mêmes,

* Le Sursis (p.155)

qui n'ont jamais été malades, qui n'ont pas de tics, qui prennent les femmes et la vie à pleines mains et qui marchent droit vers leur but en vous envoyant dinguer contre les vitrines. (*Le Sursis,* p. 24)

2. Quelle importance ils attachent, mon Dieu, à penser tous ensemble les mêmes choses. (*La Nausée,* p. 19)

Both the Negro and Lizzie in the play *La Putain Respectueuse* are victims of the *salauds;* both are outcasts, the one because he has black skin, the other because she is a prostitute. Both are paralysed into inactivity, conforming in spite of themselves to a scale of values which is not theirs. The Negro accepts that he cannot revenge himself on the white men, although he is innocent of the rape of which they have accused him, *because* he is a Negro. Lizzie cannot help him, *because* she is a whore.

Several critics have pointed out the frequency with which Sartre turns to characters who are outcasts in some fundamental way: orphans like Sartre himself, like Baudelaire, like Genet; bastards like Kean, like Goetz. Their social ostracization is the work of the *salauds.*

The victim who is described in the most lucid and persuasive detail is Jean Genet. At the age of ten, Genet is caught stealing. He is immediately labelled as 'the Thief', who has sinned against the established order and, to confirm and sustain that order, he must remain 'the thief' all his life. He is made into an object by those who control the world:

3. La honte du petit Genet lui découvre l'éternité: il est voleur de naissance, il le demeurera jusqu'à sa mort; le temps n'est qu'un songe: sa nature mauvaise s'y réfracte en mille éclats, en mille petits larcins mais elle n'appartient pas à l'ordre temporel; Genet est un voleur: voilà sa vérité, son essence éternelle. Et, s'il *est* voleur, if faut donc qu'il le soit toujours, partout: non pas seulement quand il vole, mais quand il mange, quand il dort, quand il embrasse sa mère adoptive; chacun de ses gestes le trahit, révèle au grand jour sa nature infecte: à tout moment l'instituteur peut interrompre sa dictée, regarder Genet dans les yeux

et s'écrier d'une voix forte: 'Mais voilà un voleur!' En
vain croirait-il mériter l'indulgence en avouant ses fautes,
en dominant la perversité de ses instincts: tous les mouve-
ments de son coeur sont également coupables parce que
tous expriment également son essence.

(Saint-Genet, p. 24)

It is too much to ask that anyone should try to understand
why the young Genet committed an act of theft. To understand
why would be to admit that they might be capable of theft
themselves; it is inconceivable that they should allow such an
attack on their security. Genet is labelled 'The Thief' in the
same way that the Negro in *La Putain Respectueuse* is labelled
'The Negro', Goetz in *Le Diable et le Bon Dieu* is labelled 'The
Bastard' and the Jew in Sartre's essay 'Réflexion sur la Question
Juive' is labelled 'The Jew'. Genet will henceforth be the symbol
of Larceny. The 'comédien et martyr' Genet makes his decision
to give in and conform to the role which has been imposed
upon him. He will '*be*' The Thief. But, Sartre says, he has
already lost the initiative.

The values of Good and Evil, of Right and Wrong, have been
so well instilled into little Genet that he shares them. He feels
guilt in the conviction that he has done wrong, and therefore
shares the disgust which he has inspired in the adults who con-
demn him. He connives in their destruction of him, helping
them to manufacture the product which he will become. 'Il se
déchire de ses propres mains', says Sartre, who goes on to
describe with evident anger the little boy's bewildered and
pathetic search for his own identity:

4. une malédiction, une culpabilité atroce l'écrasent: il est un
   monstre, il sent passer sur sa nuque le souffle de ce monstre,
   il se retourne et ne trouve personne; tout le monde peut
   voir l'énorme vermine, lui seul ne la voit pas. Autre que
   tous les autres, il est autre que lui-même. Enfant martyr,
   enfant public, les autres l'ont investi, pénétré, circulent en
   foule et tout à l'aise dans son âme ... Ce n'est pas un
   homme: c'est une créature de l'homme, entièrement

occupée par les hommes; on l'a produit, fabriqué de
toutes pièces.   (*Saint-Genet*, p. 49)

5. Pour faire Genet, . . . on a pris un enfant et on en a fait un
monstre pour des raisons d'utilité sociale. Si, dans cette
affaire, nous voulons trouver les vrais coupables, tournons-
nous vers les honnêtes gens et demandons-leur par quelle
étrange cruauté ils ont fait d'un enfant leur bouc émissaire.
(Ibid, p. 29)

In all Sartre's books, there is no better example of the passion
with which he detests the 'swine' who need scapegoats to bolster
up and illustrate their own proprietary rights to decide what is
permissible. Sartre himself, as a child, all but succumbed to
pressures to make of him something that he was not, and
thereby take from him his Freedom:

6. Ma vérité, mon caractère et mon nom étaient aux mains
des adultes; j'avais appris à me voir par leurs yeux;
j'étais un enfant, ce monstre qu'ils fabriquent avec leurs
regrets.   (*Les Mots*, p. 66)

E. Easy Answers

The intellectual who claims to recognize man's freedom in a
world where no absolute laws are given, and asserts therefore
that he is an end in himself, the only reality worth our attention,
might, on the face of it, appear to merit Sartre's approval.
Such a man is the Humanist. Does he not regard man as the
creator of values? Does he not thereby uphold man's inalienable freedom? But the Humanist is equally guilty, in a
way, of *mauvaise foi*, since he is striking an attitude which is
insincere. His very Humanism is an affirmation of an eternal
value known as 'Mankind'; it is an escape from the necessity
of original evaluations into the easy, comforting protection of a
ready-made value, which is 'The Dignity of Man'. For Sartre,
man has no dignity until he creates it for himself, so fine-
sounding principles such as these are empty illusions. Hoederer
accuses Hugo in *Les Mains Sales* of indulging in theoretic
ideas of man rather than being concerned with men: 'Tu

n'aimes pas les hommes, Hugo,' he says, 'tu n'aimes que les principes.' And Goetz, in *Le Diable et le Bon Dieu*, shows signs of loving Mankind but loathing men, whom he regards as beneath him. The Humanist is at best deceiving himself; at worst he is guilty of intellectual arrogance.

In fiction, Sartre's finest realization of the Humanist illusion is represented by l'Autodidacte in *La Nausée*. Roquentin comes across this grotesque puppet of a man in the Municipal Library at Bouville. After some observation, he notices that l'Autodidacte is slowly working through every book in the library in alphabetical order, with the clear assumption that when he has got to Z he will know all there is to know. And where will he go from there, wonders Roquentin, increasingly irritated. They begin conversation, and l'Autodidacte defends his Humanism:

1. Est-ce ma faute (writes Roquentin), si, dans tout ce qu'il me dit, je reconnais au passage l'emprunt, la citation? Si je vois réapparaître, pendant qu'il parle, tous les humanistes que j'ai connus? (*La Nausée*, p. 165)

2. l'humaniste qui aime les hommes tels qu'ils sont, celui qui les aime tels qu'ils devraient être, celui qui veut les sauver avec leur agrément et celui qui les sauvera malgré eux, celui qui veut créer des mythes nouveaux et celui qui se contente des anciens, celui qui aime dans l'homme sa mort, celui qui aime dans l'homme sa vie, l'humaniste joyeux, qui a toujours le mot pour rire, l'humaniste sombre, qu'on rencontre surtout aux veillées funèbres. Ils se haïssent tous entre eux: en tant qu'individus, naturellement – pas en tant qu'hommes. Mais l'Autodidacte l'ignore; il les a enfermés en lui comme des chats dans un sac de cuir et ils s'entredéchirent sans qu'il s'en aperçoive.

(Ibid, p. 166)

With swingeing mockery, Roquentin questions the Humanist on the couple sitting behind him in the library; he has not even noticed them. When Roquentin delivers his final attack on the foolish man, we discern why Sartre has so little patience with

the self-styled Humanist; he does not admire or love men at all,
he merely *pretends* to admire Man with a capital M, and therein
lies his *mauvaise foi*:

   3. Vous voyez bien que vous ne les aimez pas, ces deux-là.
      Vous ne sauriez peut-être pas les reconnaître dans la rue.
      Ce ne sont que des symboles, pour vous. Ce n'est pas du
      tout sur eux que vous êtes en train de vous attendrir; vous
      vous attendrissez sur la Jeunesse de l'Homme, sur l'Amour
      de l'Homme et de la Femme, sur la Voix humaine.
      – Eh Bien? Est-ce que ça n'existe pas?
      – Certes non, ça n'existe pas! Ni la Jeunesse, ni l'Age mûr,
      ni la Vieillesse, ni la Mort.   (*La Nausée*, pp. 169–70)

Sartre resumes this theme in *L'Existentialisme est un Humanisme*, where he again rejects the notion of Mankind as a superior,
intangible value, because such a notion in fact robs man of his
freedom to reassess, re-evaluate himself afresh in every new
situation:

   4. l'existentialiste ne prendra jamais l'homme comme fin,
      car il est toujours à faire.
                     (*L'Existentialisme est un Humanisme,* p. 92)

It might be thought that this lecture is unfortunately titled, in
view of Sartre's unequivocal rejection of Humanism, but the
author goes on to explain why he has used the word in connec-
tion with his philosophy:

   4. Il n'y a pas d'autre univers qu'un univers humain,
      l'univers de la subjectivité humaine.   (Ibid, p. 93)

The Sartrean vision of existence is only Humanistic in the sense
that it *starts from* the recognition of man's freedom, and
acknowledges no other legislator than the individual man
himself.

   The orthodox Humanist, on the other hand, alienates his
freedom by approaching every circumstance with a fixed and
static idea of 'Mankind', and submitting all his judgements to
the scrutiny of this Abstract Idea.

To conclude, *mauvaise foi* covers a multitude of devices by which men, afraid of the void which Absurdity has exposed before them, pretend to deny their *Freedom*. These devices range from blind self-deception to culpable hypocrisy. They all have as their aim to transform man into a passive material object, and so strip him of his autonomy.

There is a final variety of *mauvaise foi* which does not fit very easily into any of the categories listed. The attitude taken by Mathieu, for example, is born neither of self-deception, nor of hypocrisy. Mathieu is a lucid man, perfectly aware that human life is essentially pointless and that he is therefore free to give it a point, but he does not want to be bothered with the problem. 'A quoi bon?' he sighs. His attitude is one of indifference.

> 1. Il était plongé dans une indifférence profonde et paralysante.
>   (*L'Age de Raison*, p. 432)

In *Le Sursis* (the action of which takes place at the time of Munich), the threatening war is symbolic of the overbearing absurdity of life. Mathieu's position in face of the war is reminiscent of Pontius Pilate:

> 2. C'est une maladie, tout juste une maladie: elle est tombée sur moi par hasard, elle ne me concerne pas, il faut la traiter par le stoïcisme comme la goutte ou les maux de dents.
>   (*Le Sursis*, p. 391)

We have spent some time examining the ways in which men deny their freedom, since Sartre is most eloquent in attacking them. We must now return to consider what men *should* do with the dreadful power that has been revealed to them.

4

Choice and Responsibility

A. Choice

Thrown into a contingent world which is not of his making, denied the props of eternal values to support him, man is alone, unjustified, and irremediably free. How will he exercise this freedom? By constantly interpreting and re-interpreting the world around him, by making fresh judgements in every new situation, and, above all, by an ever-renewed effort of *self-justification*.

This implies that he must constantly make *choices* between various possible courses of behaviour. In his total liberty, he can only give significance to the world and justification to himself by the choices he makes and by the definitions he invents; he will define himself by his choices.

Thus, we arrive at another paradox, which is this: man has not *chosen* to be free, yet his freedom obliges him to *choose* how to use it. Freedom involves the necessity of choice, which is the activity by which man exercises and demonstrates his *autonomy*. Against the famous initial truth of Descartes, *cogito, ergo sum*, one might almost propose a parallel existential truth, which would be *eligo, ergo sum*: it is by virtue of the obligation to choose that man is differentiated from the viscous mess of static objects.

So, if man is free to invent meanings for himself and for the world, he is, at the same time, obliged to invent them; there is no escape from Choice.

Even the cowards who throw in the sponge, who strive to

abstain from this choice, are still choosing, in a way; their very abstention, their *mauvaise foi*, is an act of choosing.

It is not possible, then, *not* to choose. Man's destiny is in his own hands; it will be defined by the way in which he *chooses himself*:

1. le choix libre que l'homme fait de soi-même s'identifie absolument avec ce qu'on appelle sa destinée.

   (*Baudelaire,* p. 245)

2. Chaque personnage ne sera rien que le choix d'une issue et ne vaudra pas plus que l'issue choisie. . . . Une issue, ça s'invente. Et chacun, en inventant sa propre issue, s'invente soi-même. L'homme est à inventer chaque jour.

   (*Qu'est-ce que la littérature?*, p. 352)

If man is condemned to justify himself by the choices he makes, by his perpetual re-creation of values, it follows once more that there can be no Good and Evil as absolutes; they are concepts which must be relative to each situation, and which are impossible to tabulate before that situation occurs. Morals are not, then, to be observed in a blind obedience to a code, but in the free and conscious expression of autonomous Choice.

Baudelaire is therefore immoral in the Sartrean sense as well as being immoral in the Christian sense. His Christian immorality consists in his purposefully committing Evil while retaining a notion of the Good. His Sartrean immorality is far worse: it consists in accepting these notions of Good and Evil as absolute, and refusing to exercise his freedom by choosing his own Good and Evil.

For the same reason, Sartre finds Cartesian freedom unsatisfactory. Descartes starts from the same premise as Sartre, namely that the world is contingent and meaningless and that man is thereby rendered free, but he later maintains that since he has a 'clear and distinct idea' of the Good, goodness must exist *a priori*, and must come from God. Hence, man's freedom is limited within the framework of an established morality, and his choice can only be a negative one:

2. C'est que Descartes, savant dogmatique et bon chrétien, se laisse écraser par l'ordre préétabli des vérités éternelles et par le système éternel des valeurs créées par Dieu. S'il n'invente pas son Bien, s'il ne construit pas la Science, l'homme n'est plus libre que nominalement. Et la liberté cartésienne rejoint ici la liberté chrétienne, qui est une fausse liberté: l'homme cartésien, l'homme chrétien sont libres pour le Mal, non pour le Bien, pour l'Erreur, non pour la Vérité. Dieu, par le concours des lumières naturelles et surnaturelles qu'il leur dispense, les conduit par la main vers la Connaissance et la Vertu qu'il a choisies pour eux; ils n'ont qu'à se laisser faire; tout le mérite de cette ascension lui reviendra.   (*Situations I*, p. 330)

Thus, Descartes's freedom is reduced to a purely negative freedom; the possibility of an active choice is denied, there remains only the possibility of refusing the choices which God has already made, and going no further:

3. Puisque l'ordre des vérités existe en dehors de moi, ce qui va me définir comme autonomie, ce n'est pas l'invention créatrice, c'est le refus. C'est en refusant jusqu'à ce que nous ne puissions plus refuser que nous sommes libres.
          (Ibid, p. 326)

At the end of *La Nausée*, Roquentin has acknowledged his Freedom, but has not yet made a positive choice to justify his own life.

Daniel, in *Les Chemins de la Liberté*, makes his choice in agreeing to play the role of the Homosexual as the Other sees him, while Genet agrees to play the role of the Thief. Both choices, as we have seen in the last chapter, are mistaken, since they are not the expression of one's own Freedom so much as submission to the Freedom of the Other.

Mathieu in *Les Chemins de la Liberté* makes his choice when he opens fire on the German tormentors, and Oreste makes his in killing Egisthe and Clytemnestra *for his own reasons* rather than for reasons of vengeance.

Man is distinguished from the material world by virtue of his power to choose freely. Things simply *are*, without effort. Man must not *be* as a Thing is, he must *exist*, and it will require much effort to transcend from 'being', which is a state, to 'existing', which is an ever-moving, constant rebirth. This transcendence can only be achieved by the Choice, which is consequently as much a burden to be borne as a release from stagnancy to be welcomed.

> 4. vous êtes libres; choisissez, c'est-à-dire inventez. Aucune morale générale ne peut vous indiquer ce qu'il y a à faire; il n'y a pas de signe dans le monde.
>
> (*L'Existentialisme est un Humanisme*, p. 47)

B. Responsibility

The obligation to make choices every day of one's life is all the more burdensome when one realizes that one is not only choosing for oneself but for the whole of mankind. The act of choosing thus carries with it an enormous *responsibility*, both to oneself and to the totality of men. When a man invents his own values, his own morals, he is creating a standard which must of necessity implicate other men. If, for example, a man chooses to marry his brother's widow to provide her with companionship for the remainder of her life, he is inventing a course of action which other men in similar situations may follow, or may not follow. Whether they follow it or not, the example has been offered to them, and a value has been suggested to them. The attitude of the man who creates an example therefore implicates other men's attitudes, and he is responsible not only to himself, but to them also. By implicitly proposing that they *should* act in the way that he has acted, he carries on his own shoulders the responsibility of having created a new value.

Furthermore, his act of choosing makes man responsible for the future. In severing his ties with the past, with established models of behaviour, man is making of himself a *project* who will give meaning to himself and to the world *in the future*.

This is why, in Sartrean ontology, man cannot be said to 'be' (as a stone 'is'), but to 'become'.

The clearest explanation of what is meant by responsibility is given by Sartre in *L'Existentialisme est un Humanisme*:

1. Mais si vraiment l'existence précède l'essence, l'homme est responsable de ce qu'il est. Ainsi, la première démarche de l'existentialisme est de mettre tout homme en possession de ce qu'il est et de faire reposer sur lui la responsabilité totale de son existence. Et, quand nous disons que l'homme est responsable de lui-même, nous ne voulons pas dire que l'homme est responsable de sa stricte individualité, mais qu'il est responsable de tous les hommes. (p. 24)

2. Quand nous disons que l'homme se choisit, nous entendons que chacun d'entre nous se choisit, mais par là nous voulons dire aussi qu'en se choisissant il choisit tous les hommes. En effet, il n'y a pas un de nos actes qui, en créant l'homme que nous voulons être, ne crée en même temps une image de l'homme tel que nous estimons qu'il doit être. Choisir d'être ceci ou cela, c'est affirmer en même temps la valeur de ce que nous choississons, car nous ne pouvons jamais choisir le mal . . . (p. 25)

3. Ainsi, notre responsabilité est beaucoup plus grande que nous ne pourrions le supposer, car elle engage l'humanité entière. (p. 26)

4. je suis obligé à chaque instant de faire des actes exemplaires. (p. 31)

5. l'existentialiste, lorsqu'il décrit un lâche, dit que ce lâche est responsable de sa lâcheté. . . . il s'est construit comme lâche par ses actes. (pp. 59–60)

In his vast psycho-analytic study of the writer Jean Genet, Sartre discusses this theme of responsibility in greater depth. He points out that by *choosing*, in full consciousness, to be a pederast and a thief, Genet chose these possibilities for mankind, and bears the responsibility of having proposed, simply by his choice, the value of pederasty for all. Genet does not speak *about* the homosexual, but *as* a homosexual; the possibility of homosexuality is thereby subjectivized, removed from the comfortable position of being an object perceived by the consciousness into that of a possible choice of the consciousness; if Genet can choose to be a homosexual, anyone can make such a choice:

6. si la pédérastie est le choix d'une conscience, elle devient une possibilité humaine. L'*homme* est pédéraste, voleur et traitre. Il est *aussi*, bien sûr, hétérosexuel, honnête et fidèle. Le dogmatisme antique concluait: puisqu'il peut être honnête ou voleur, c'est qu'il n'est ni l'un ni l'autre. Il en résultait que l'homme n'était rien. Pour la pensée contemporaine, qui cherche le concret historique, l'humanité concrète est la totalité de ses contradictions. Puisqu'il y a des amours licites, il y a une possibilité humaine de refuser ces amours et de chercher le vice. Inversement, puisqu'il y a des vices, les amours licites deviennent normales. . . .
      . . . toute aventure humaine, quelque singulière qu'elle puisse paraître, engage l'humanité entière . . .
      . . . nous reconnaissons dans l'horreur un *sujet*, il est notre vérité comme nous sommes la sienne; nos vertus et ses crimes sont interchangeables.
                                        (*Saint Genet,* pp. 339–40)

At the end of *La Nausée*, Roquentin's feeling of responsibility is barely embryonic, and applies only on a personal, individual level; he is aware that he is responsible for himself. Oreste, however, is aware that he is responsible on a universal level; in choosing his own way in defiance of Jupiter, he takes upon himself the burden of responsibility for the entire population of Argos. The practical consequences implied by a strict adherence to this concept are, of course, staggering; the fact that Jean-Paul Sartre himself does not shrink from them lends ever greater authority to the quality of his thought.

5
Action

The obligation to make choices and accept responsibility for those choices is an obligation which is ceaselessly renewed and ever-present. As Sartre has said, 'L'homme est à inventer chaque jour.' It is by the choices he makes that he will resolve the dilemma of his existence. *Choice, responsibility, invention,* all point to the fact that it is impossible to describe a man according to the attributes he possesses; he cannot have a *personality* composed of acquired characteristics. Since he is constantly *inventing himself* he can only be described in terms of what he does, of what he makes of himself. In short, he is knowable only by his actions:

1. L'homme, tel que le conçoit l'existentialiste, s'il n'est pas définissable, c'est qu'il n'est d'abord rien. Il ne sera qu'-ensuite, et il sera tel qu'il se sera fait. Ainsi, il n'y a pas de nature humaine, puisqu'il n'y a pas de Dieu pour la concevoir. L'homme est seulement, non seulement tel qu'il se conçoit, mais tel qu'il se veut, et comme il se conçoit après l'existence, comme il se veut après cet élan vers l'existence; l'homme n'est rien d'autre que ce qu'il se fait. Tel est le premier principe de l'existentialisme.
   (*L'Existentialisme est un Humanisme,* p. 22)

Meaningful acts, taken in full consciousness of absolute liberty, are the only road towards relieving the world of its contingent absurdity:

2. La doctrine que je vous présente est justement à l'opposé du quiétisme, puisqu'elle déclare: il n'y a de réalité que dans l'action; elle va plus loin d'ailleurs, puisqu'elle ajoute: l'homme n'est rien d'autre que son projet, il

n'existe que dans la mesure où il se réalise, il n'est donc rien d'autre que l'ensemble de ses actes.   (Ibid, p. 55)

It is perhaps as well, at this point, to recall the quotation from *Baudelaire* (p. 49) which we have given earlier, and which re-iterates the notion of man constructing his own essence by his actions:

3. Peut-être on n'*est* pas pour soi-même à la manière d'une chose. Peut-être même qu'on n'*est* pas du tout: toujours en question, toujours en sursis, peut-être doit-on per-pétuellement se *faire*.

The italics are Sartre's, and the implications of doubt refer, of course, to Baudelaire's self-questioning, not to Sartre's.

The emphasis on *action*, on *doing things,* is a matter of cardinal importance to Sartre's conception of man. It is not enough for us to recognize *intellectually* our freedom and responsibility and then to resume the lives we have hitherto been leading in bad faith. Sartrean freedom and choice are not freedom to think what we like or to choose what we believe. The freedom is freedom to *behave* authentically without reference to the past, to the Other, or to abstract concepts; the choice is a choice between different *actions*. One can understand why Sartre is impatient with Cartesian freedom, which is finally little more than freedom of thought, or of opinion. I have already discussed Sartre's opposition to Descartes's moral system, which implicitly postulates the existence of an eternal legislator. His opposition to the Cartesian method of doubt is even more dismissive, since the freedom it produces, says Sartre, is merely intellectual and consequently *useless*:

4. C'est une chose, en effet, d'éprouver qu'on est libre sur le plan de l'action, de l'entreprise sociale ou politique, de la création dans les arts, et une autre chose de l'éprouver dans l'acte de comprendre et de découvrir.
   (*Situations I*, p. 314)

5. l'expérience première (de Descartes) n'est pas celle de la

> liberté créatrice 'ex nihilo', mais d'abord celle de la
> pensée autonome qui découvre par ses propres forces des
> relations intelligibles entre des essences déjà existantes.
> C'est pourquoi, nous autres Français qui vivons depuis
> trois siècles sur la liberté cartésienne, nous entendons
> implicitement par 'libre arbitre' l'exercice d'une *pensée*
> indépendante plutôt que la production d'un acte créateur,
> et finalement nos philosophes assimilent, comme Alain, la
> liberté avec l'acte de juger.   (Ibid, p. 315)

Freedom to think, to know, to understand, is for-ever turned in
upon itself. It is not *productive*, it cannot create anything *new*,
whereas for Sartre, man must always be engaged in the task of
renewing himself. It is significant that the Cartesian method is
arrived at through the process of dispassionate, mathematical
logic, while Sartre's ontological conclusions derive from an
initial intense feeling of repugnance with the contingent world,
and passionate anger at its calm insolence. The two men could
not be more opposed. Descartes is a mathematician. Sartre, as
both Maurice Cranston and Iris Murdoch have pointed out, is a
Romantic. The truths which a mathematician may glean by the
application of his mind do not interest Sartre, because they are
irrelevant to the problem of existence:

> 6. Tout est fixé: l'objet à découvrir et la méthode. L'enfant
> qui applique sa liberté à faire une addition selon les règles
> n'enrichit pas l'univers d'une vérité nouvelle; il ne fait
> que recommencer une opération que mille autres ont faite
> avant lui et qu'il ne pourra jamais mener plus loin qu'eux.
> C'est donc un paradoxe assez frappant que l'attitude du
> mathématicien; et son esprit est semblable à un homme
> qui, engagé dans un sentier fort étroit où chacun de ses pas
> et la position même de son corps seraient rigoureusement
> conditionnés par la nature du sol et les nécessités de la
> marche, serait pourtant pénétré par l'inébranlable con-
> viction d'accomplir librement tous ses actes.
>   (Ibid, p. 316)

Hugo in *Les Mains Sales* is an intellectual Communist who
thinks rather than *acts*. Assigned by the Party to liquidate

Hoederer, who is suspected of treason to the Party's principles, he continually procrastinates, is all the time assailed by thoughts. In conversation with Hoederer, he says:

7. HUGO: Il y a beaucoup de pensées dans ma tête. Il faut que je les chasse.

HOEDERER: Quel genre de pensées?

HUGO: Qu'est-ce que je fais ici? Est-ce que j'ai raison de vouloir ce que je veux? Est-ce que je ne suis pas en train de jouer la comédie? Des trucs comme ça ... Il faut que je me défende. Que j'installe d'autres pensées dans ma tête. Des consignes: 'Fais ceci. Marche. Arrête-toi. Dis cela.' J'ai besoin d'obéir. Obéir et c'est tout. Manger, dormir, obéir.

Hugo's dilemma is that of any intellectual radical. He has asserted his freedom by joining the party, presumably against all the inherited values of his upbringing and class, yet he is not truly free until he has *done* something; actions are not generally the province of the intellectual, bourgeois or otherwise. Thoughts are their defence and their raison d'être. They must eventually act, however, not by obedience, as Hugo here suggests, but through a need to commit some original, authentic action to bear visible witness to the choice they have made for themselves. 'Tous les intellectuels rêvent de faire de l'action', says Hoederer. And Mathieu: 'Je ne sais pas ce que je donnerais pour faire un acte irrémédiable.' (*L'Age de Raison,* p. 439).

Man will never *define himself* or *justify himself* with thoughts, however honest. An irremediable act is the only method by which he can give himself any meaning. After his double assassination, Oreste confronts the people of Argos with the words:

8. vous avez compris que mon crime est bien à moi; je le revendique à la face du soleil, il est ma raison de vivre et mon orgueil, vous ne pouvez pas ni me châtier, ni me plaindre, et c'est pourquoi je vous fais peur.

(Les Mouches)

Oreste has found himself through action, in his case murder. It might not have been murder, it might have been some other act. All that matters is that it should be an act committed through free choice, without accounting to any ordained value.

It remains only to decide what *kind* of action we are to commit. We shall consider three possibilities postulated in Sartre's work, and rejected by him:

> A. Should we wilfully commit acts which we know to be wrong, which challenge the dictates of established morality?
>
> B. Should we commit suicide in order to express our freedom and as a means of awakening our fellow-men to the absurdity of their existence?
>
> C. Should we indulge in Gidean[1] 'actes gratuits' in order to show that we are free to do whatever we like?

A. Immorality

Sartre's most complete study of a consciously immoral life is contained in his psychological analysis of Baudelaire's 'conscience dans le Mal'. Sartre's position is briefly this: in order to use his freedom to justify his existence, Baudelaire makes his Choice. In a conscious decision at a turning-point in his life, Baudelaire chooses Evil. He will devote his life to the pursuit of immorality. Sartre's contention is that this is not, however, a truly free choice, since Baudelaire continues to regard his immoral acts as immoral:

> 1. Entendons bien qu'il ne s'agit pas de cueillir les fruits défendus *quoiqu'ils* soient défendus, mais *parce qu'ils* sont défendus.   (*Baudelaire*, p. 86)

[1] *Andre Gide* (1869–1951) One of the most prolific of French writers, Gide's output spans more than half a century. Comparatively early in his career, he developed the idea of *l'acte gratuit*, a motiveless and irrational act which would be without purpose or profit, and would express personal liberty. Examples of this idea are to be found in, amongst other works, *Les Caves du Vatican* (1914).

By recognizing that his acts are wrong, Baudelaire is giving silent approbation to the notion that there is an *a priori* conception of what is right:

> 2. Faire le Mal pour le Mal c'est très exactement faire tout exprès le contraire de ce que l'on continue d'affirmer comme le Bien. (Ibid, p. 87)

Sartre compares the attitude of Baudelaire with that of a high priest in a black mass, and contrasts it with that of the true atheist. The atheist, he says, spares no thought for God, as He does not exist. The black mass preacher, on the other hand, hates God because He is good, and his hatred is helping to affirm the order which he professes to despise. The black mass preacher hates God, and thereby implies that God must exist in order to be hated. Baudelaire commits evil acts with the implication that there are good acts to be committed, which he has rejected. His solitude is not therefore complete, and does not engage the sympathy or approval of Sartre:

> 3. Et celui qui se damne acquiert une solitude qui est comme l'image affaiblie de la grande solitude de l'homme vraiment libre. Il est seul, en effet, tout autant qu'il le veut, pas plus. (Ibid, p. 88–9)

Baudelaire's immorality is, then, a cowardly flight from the responsibility of a truly free choice. Unable to face the anguish of absolute solitude in a world without values, he adheres to established moral codes. Further, he tries to define himself in terms of these moral codes, to invest himself with an essence, a description. He will be 'the man who is immoral'. Clothed in this description, he will be as an object in front of the Other, and will continue to illustrate his self-imposed description, confirmed by the Other, by further immoral acts. He will always rest in the comforting knowledge that he 'is' something, as a tree is a tree. Baudelaire is in this way guilty, in Sartrean terminology, of *mauvaise foi*:

> 4. Cette âme singulière vit dans la mauvaise foi. Il y a en

effet en elle quelque chose qu'elle se dissimule dans une fuite perpétuelle: c'est qu'elle a choisi de ne pas choisir *son* Bien, c'est que sa liberté profonde, renaclant devant elle-même, emprunte au-dehors des principes tout faits, précisément parce qu'ils sont tout faits.   (Ibid, p. 100)

The evidence that Baudelaire retains a conception of predetermined Good and Evil is contained in his ceaseless feeling of culpability. I have pointed out in the chapter on *mauvaise foi* that Baudelaire's remorse is an aspect of his search for the past; Sartre further suggests that the immorality is born of a *need* to feel guilty; Baudelaire commits evil in order, it seems, to repent it immediately afterwards:

> 5. Ayant opté pour le mal, il a choisi de se sentir coupable. C'est à travers le remords qu'il réalise son unicité et sa liberté de pécheur. De toute sa vie, le sentiment de sa culpabilité ne le quittera pas ... le remords a chez lui une importance fonctionnelle. C'est lui qui fait de l'acte un péché; un crime dont on ne se repent pas n'est plus un crime, mais tout au plus une malchance. Il semble même que, chez lui, le remords ait précédé la faute. ... Il a une si violente horreur de lui-même qu'on peut considérer sa vie comme une longue suite de punitions qu'il s'inflige.
>
> (Ibid, p. 102–3)

A free man cannot sin, because he does not recognize that there is anything to sin against. Oreste, in *Les Mouches*, will show no remorse for his act of murder, because he does not recognize it as a crime. He is truly a free man. Baudelaire, on the contrary, in acting against established value, implicitly maintains, by his remorse, that there are such values to act against. Immorality is not, therefore, a valid Choice for a free man to make.

Goetz, in *Le Diable et le Bon Dieu*, is a character allied in conception to Sartre's view of Baudelaire. At the beginning of the play, he commits evil for the sake of evil. He then reverts completely, and commits Good for its own sake also. By the end of the play, he has realized that he has all the time been trying to clothe himself with an essence composed of recognizable attributes, first the qualities of the evil man, then the qualities of the saint. He now knows that these qualities do not exist since there is, after all, no God to invent them. Man must invent them for himself:

> 6. Je me demandais à chaque minute ce que je pouvais être aux yeux de Dieu. A présent, je connais la réponse! rien. Dieu ne me voit pas. Dieu ne m'entend pas, Dieu ne me connaît pas ... Le silence, c'est Dieu. L'absence, c'est Dieu Dieu, c'est la solitude des hommes. Si Dieu existe, l'homme est néant; si l'homme existe ... Heinrich, je vais te faire connaître une espièglerie considérable: Dieu n'existe pas.

Having rejected both immorality and saintlihood, Goetz will henceforth be completely free to invent his own system of meanings, to create his own justification for existence. He *is* nothing; he *will be* Freedom itself.

B. Suicide

Lucien, the hero of the short story *L'Enfance d'un Chef*, contemplates suicide as an act which will both be irrevocable, and will awaken people to the futility of their lives:

> 1. On ne pouvait pas compter sur un traité de philosophie pour persuader aux gens qu'ils n'existaient pas. Ce qu'il fallait, c'était un acte, un acte vraiment désespéré qui dissipât les apparences et montrât en pleine lumière le néant du monde. Une détonation, un jeune corps saignant sur un tapis, quelques mots griffonnés sur une feuille: 'Je me tue parce que je n'existe pas. Et vous aussi, mes frères, vous êtes néant!' Les gens liraient leur journal le matin; ils verraient: 'Un adolescent a osé!' Et chacun se sentirait terriblement troublé et se demanderait: 'Et moi? Est-ce que j'existe?'   (*Le Mur*, p. 179)

Baudelaire, we find, considered suicide a possible issue from his anguish. His death would stabilize his essence into a collection of memories, so that he would no longer have the onerous responsibility of creating himself by his acts:

2. S'affirmer, pour Baudelaire, c'est en effet se poser comme pure essence inactive, c'est-à-dire au fond, comme une mémoire; et se nier, c'est vouloir n'être, une fois pour toutes, que la chaine irrémédiable de ses souvenirs.

(*Baudelaire,* p. 241)

Yet another instance of the frame of mind which can consider suicide occurs in *Les Chemins de la Liberté.* Mathieu is weary of life and of his isolation; he is standing on a bridge overlooking the Seine:

3. Le repos. Pourquoi pas? Ce suicide obscur ce serait aussi un absolu. Toute une loi, tout un choix, toute une morale. Un acte unique, incomparable qui illuminerait une seconde le pont et la Seine. Il suffirait de se pencher un peu plus et il se serait choisi pour l'éternité. Il se pencha, mais ses mains ne lâchaient pas la pierre, elles supportaient tout le poids de son corps. Pourquoi pas? Il n'avait pas de raison particulière pour se laisser couler, mais il n'avait pas non plus de raison pour s'en empêcher. Et l'acte était là, devant lui, sur l'eau noire, il lui dessinait son avenir.

(*Le Sursis,* pp. 420–1)

Sartre has given his final answer on the possibility of suicide in *L'Être et le Néant.* Having pointed out that death removes all hope of meaning from life, he continues:

4. Le suicide ne saurait être considéré comme une fin de vie dont je serais le propre fondement. Étant acte de ma vie, en effet, il requiert lui-même une signification que seul l'avenir peut lui donner; mais comme il est le *dernier* acte de ma vie, il se refuse cet avenir; ainsi demeure-t-il totalement indéterminé. Si j'échappe à la mort, en effet, ou si je 'me manque', ne jugerai-je pas plus tard mon suicide comme une lâcheté? L'événement ne pourra-t-il pas me montrer que d'autres solutions étaient possibles? Mais comme ces solutions ne peuvent être que mes propres projets, elles ne peuvent apparaître que si je vis. Le suicide est une absurdité qui fait sombrer ma vie dans l'absurde.

(*L'Être et le Néant,* p. 624)

Suicide is not an acceptable choice

(*a*) because it creates an essence which is fixed in the past. The suicide can only be defined by the memory of what he *was*. No further actions are possible in the future. The suicide therefore assumes by his act all the passivity of a Thing.

(*b*) because, far from releasing the world from its crushing absurdity, it merely compounds it. The suicide accepts that the world is meaningless, but refuses to give it meaning; instead of striving to construct order out of chaos, he adds to the chaos.

C. Actes Gratuits

It might seem that an *acte gratuit*, in the sense that André Gide understood the phrase, could be a perfect expression of freedom. To do things without any rational foundation, without recourse to any motive or purpose, could not such behaviour constitute a Choice which would assert Freedom with some insolence? Sartre's reply is unequivocally negative. He gives the example of Mathieu, who, in *Les Chemins de la Liberté*, resorts to such motiveless actions to demonstrate that he is free. For instance, he sticks a knife into his own hand (*L'Age de Raison*, p. 285). An act of this kind may be free, but it is irresponsible, and cannot, therefore, have any validity for Sartre. An *acte gratuit* contributes in no way to the definition or justification of a man, it only indulges his whim:

1. et si l'on croit retrouver ici la théorie gidienne de l'acte gratuit, c'est qu'on ne voit pas l'énorme différence entre cette doctrine et celle de Gide. Gide ne sait pas ce que c'est qu'une situation; il agit par simple caprice. Pour nous, au contraire, l'homme se trouve dans une situation organisée, où il est lui-même engagé, il engage par son choix l'humanité entière, et il ne peut pas éviter de choisir.

(*L'Existentialisme est un Humanisme*, p. 74)

Boris, in *Le Sursis*, makes his decision whether or not to go to war on the flip of a coin:

2. Eh bien! Je pars, dit-il à son image. Non parce que je hais la guerre, non parce que je hais ma famille, non pas même parce que j'ai décidé de partir: par pur hasard, parce qu'une pièce a roulé d'un côté plutôt que de l'autre. Admirable, pensa-t-il: je suis à l'extrême pointe de la liberté. Le martyr gratuit. (*Le Sursis*, p. 319)

Such an act is a mere mockery of freedom, adding to the gratuity of existence instead of injecting some meaning or worth into it.

Another character who adheres to the Gidean idea is Anny, the mistress of Roquentin rather sketchily portrayed in *La Nausée*. She believes that, in spite of the general absurdity of life, there are certain moments when life takes a form and a meaning, and it is these moments that she must wait for. She calls them 'des moments parfaits'. She re-appears in the novel later only to divulge that she has decided she was wrong; 'moments parfaits' do not exist after all.

An *acte gratuit* does not take into account the burden of responsibility which falls upon man to create meaning or to invent justifications. In this sense, 'Sartre is infinitely more 'moral' a writer than Gide, reminding men, as he does, of their constant need, even duty, to do meaningful acts.

A. Immorality

B. Suicide

C. Actes gratuits

These are all *individual* actions, concerned only with the person who does them. Moreover, they are all *ineffective*; the first implicitly confirms the order which it purports to overthrow, the second dispenses with any necessity to perform any further action, the third absolves itself from doing anything which is meaningful. All three modes of behaviour are unacceptable to Sartre, for whom an act must be first effective, and second responsible. And this responsibility, we recall, is a responsibility not only to oneself, but to all men.

The action which will fulfil all requirements, which will be free, meaningful, responsible, and will contribute to the *a posteriori* definition of man, is *commitment*, what Sartre has made famous with the word *l'Engagement*. Commitment demands that one should take action which involves the fate of men, and especially the fate of one's contemporaries. The well-being of men living *now* should be the object of any act committed to the definition of justification of life on this earth. Action such as this involves sinking one's own personality completely into the task of creating Man; it demands more of one than any existing code of honour or moral catechism could possibly demand.

6

L'Engagement

We must first remember that the responsibility of men to give a meaning to the world is stated by Sartre as a *fact*. One cannot choose to be responsible or not responsible; the choice lies in the way in which that responsibility will be expressed. Sartre quotes Pascal (from whom he is ethically descended): 'Nous sommes embarqués', and continues:

> 1. Si tout homme est embarqué cela ne veut point dire qu'il en ait pleine conscience; la plupart passe leur temps à se dissimuler leur engagement.
>
> (*Qu'est-ce que la Littérature,* p. 77)

One is 'engagé', then, whether one likes it or not. The cowards who people the pages of Sartrean literature in such profusion are just as 'engagé' as the active political radical, but they hide their 'engagement', reject it. One sees a slight semantic difference here between 'engagement', as Sartre understands it, and the most usual English equivalent, commitment. For Sartre, commitment does not really arise until one *accepts* one's 'engagement' and devotes oneself accordingly to *action*.

What sort of action would effectively demonstrate man's responsibility to himself and to his fellows? More particularly, what sort of action is open to the bourgeois intellectual, such as Roquentin, such as Mathieu, such as Sartre himself?

A. La Création Artistique

In the closing pages of *La Nausée*, Roquentin believes he has found the answer. He has discovered the way to give sense to the world, namely through artistic creation. He listens intently to a blues singer and a saxophonist, and concludes that they are, by their art, endowing existence with a meaning, a sense which it did not before possess:

1. Elle chante. En voilà deux   sont sauvés: le Juif et la Négresse. Sauvés. Ils se so   être crus perdus jusqu'-au bout, noyés dans l'ex   ence ... ils se sont lavés du péché d'exister. ... La Négresse chante. Alors on peut justifier son existence?   (*La Nausée*, pp. 247–8)

Roquentin decides that the action he will take will be to write a book, not a work of history, such as the biography of the Marquis de Rollebon which he had come to Bouville to complete, (because 'jamais un existant ne peut justifier l'existence d'un autre existant'), but something new and different. 'Il faudrait qu'elle soit belle et dure comme de l'acier et qu'elle fasse honte aux gens de leur existence' (ibid, p. 249). One may surmise that this is precisely what Sartre achieved with *La Nausée*.

Just as the blues singer 'saves herself' by singing, so Sartre 'saved' himself by writing. It was his means of accepting responsibility for himself, his way of 'doing' something.

2. Ma seule affaire était de me sauver – rien dans les mains, rien dans les poches – par le travail et la foi. Du coup ma pure option ne m'élevait au-dessus de personne; sans équipement, sans outillage je me suis mis tout entier à l'oeuvre pour me sauver tout entier.

                      (*Les Mots*, p. 212)

Sartre made a conscious choice to justify his existence by writing, by literary creation. Up to that moment, he had been, with some reluctance, playing the role of the prodigiously intelligent child whom everyone liked; he had been seeing himself in the eyes of the Other, and had lived passively. Writing released him from the imprisonment of an unjustified existence, became his form of action and his method of commitment. With *La Nausée* (1938), *Le Mur* (1939), and *Les Chemins de la Liberté* (1943/9), Sartre affirms the absurdity of the world and tries to make his readers aware of the emptiness of their own existence by showing in novel form the various ways in which freedom is rejected or misused. These fictitious illustrations are supported by his major theoretic treatise *L'Être et le Néant* (1943), and by plays which have had varying success.

Still later, Sartre formulates his ideas of the ways in which literary creation may be regarded properly as 'action'. In the second volume of *Situations*, which includes *Qu'est-ce que la Littérature?*, Sartre explains that literature can be a form of 'engagement', open to the intellectual who may otherwise be inactive, providing that it is concerned with *actuality*, with the *present situation*:

3. Je dirai qu'un écrivain est engagé lorsqu'il tâche à prendre la conscience la plus lucide et la plus entière d'être embarqué.   (*Qu'est-ce que la Littérature?*, p. 98)

4. Puisque l'écrivain n'a aucun moyen de s'évader, nous voulons qu'il embrasse étroitement son époque; elle est sa chance unique: elle s'est faite pour lui et il s'est fait pour elle. On regrette l'indifférence de Balzac devant les journées de 48, l'incompréhension apeurée de Flaubert en face de la Commune; on les regrette *pour eux*: il y a là .quelque chose qu'ils ont manqué pour toujours. Nous ne voulons rien manquer de notre temps: peut-être en est-il de plus beaux, mais c'est le nôtre; nous n'avons que *cette* vie à vivre, au milieu de *cette* guerre, de *cette* révolution peut-être.   (*Situations II*, p. 12)

5. Nous sommes convaincus, au contraire, qu'on ne *peut pas* tirer son épingle du jeu. Serions-nous muets et cois comme des cailloux, notre passivité même serait une action. Celui qui consacrerait sa vie à faire des romans sur des Hittites, son abstention serait par elle-même une prise de position. L'écrivain est en *situation* dans son époque; chaque parole a des retentissements. Chaque silence aussi. Je tiens Flaubert et Goncourt pour responsables pour la

répression qui suivit la Commune parce qu'ils n'ont pas écrit une ligne pour l'empêcher. Ce n'était pas leur affaire, dirait-on. Mais le procès de Calas, était-ce l'affaire de Voltaire? La condamnation de Dreyfus, était-ce l'affaire de Zola? L'administration du Congo, était-ce l'affaire de Gide? Chacun de ces auteurs, en une circonstance particulière de sa vie, a mesuré sa responsabilité d'écrivain.

(*Ibid*, p. 13)

It can be seen that Sartre has no time for critics of the past, for historians, for poets. There is no cemetery like a library, he says, and the writer who evaluates or comments upon past events cannot be considered 'engagé' because 'les abus qu'ils dénonçaient ne sont plus de notre temps' (p. 39). They contribute in no way to the justification of man as he is *now*. Hence Roquentin abandons his useless plan to write the biography of the Marquis de Rollebon.

It becomes clear, also, that writing alone is not enough. Sartre admonishes Baudelaire for his 'passive lucidity', for the fact that he chose to write not in order to contribute to the justification of man, but simply to indulge his own sense of sin. Literary creation became, for him, an end in itself; it was not an *action* which took account of his responsibility. Just as Sartre finds fault with Flaubert and Goncourt in the passage quoted above for not having spoken out against the Commune, so he reproaches Baudelaire for having 'tiré son épingle du jeu':

6. mais ce créateur ne crée plus; il rapetasse. Cent déménagements, et pas un voyage; il n'a même pas la force de s'installer à Honfleur; les évènements sociaux glissent sur lui sans le toucher. Il s'est un peu agité en 1848: mais il n'a manifesté aucun intérêt sincère pour la Révolution.

(*Baudelaire,* p. 208)

The real business of the writer is first to come to grips with his *situation* (that is, his social environment, the place and the time in which he lives), and then to exhort his readers to take action which will improve the conditions of life revealed by that *situation*.

7. Il n'est plus temps de *décrire* ni de *narrer*: nous ne pouvons pas non plus nous borner à *expliquer*. La description, fût-elle psychologique, est pure jouissance contemplative; l'explication est acceptation, elle excuse tout; l'une et l'autre supposent que les jeux sont faits. Mais si la perception même est action, si, pour nous, montrer le monde c'est toujours le dévoiler dans les perspectives d'un changement possible, alors, dans cette époque de fatalisme nous avons à révéler au lecteur, en chaque cas concret, sa puissance de faire et de défaire, bref, d'agir. (*Qu'est-ce que la Littérature?*, pp. 349–50)

The writer cannot, then, be an impartial chronicler; he must take sides, in order to reveal to his readers their possibility of choice and of action, to 'mettre la personne humaine en possession de sa liberté' (Ibid, p. 335).

There is a progression discernible from the effort of writing for personal salvation (as Roquentin contemplates at the end of *La Nausée*, and as Sartre admits to having intended at the beginning of his literary career), to a more complete involvement with the salvation of the whole of mankind. *Engagement* comes to mean political and social action:

8. la situation historique nous incite à nous joindre au prolétariat pour construire une société sans classes.
(Ibid, p. 332)

9. un écrivain peut et doit se ranger du côté de la révolution s'il est prouvé qu'il n'y a pas d'autre moyen de faire cesser une oppression. (Ibid, p. 319)

Commitment is, finally, commitment to the idea of a classless society, and the advocacy of such methods as might contribute towards its achievement. In the words of Francis Jeanson:

10. travailler parmi les hommes à la libération de tous les hommes. Il ne s'agit plus de révolte mais de révolution.
(*Sartre par lui-même*, p. 34)

This is precisely the position taken by Oreste, whose action not only justifies his own existence, but liberates the people of

Argos. Apart from Sartre himself, Oreste remains the best example in the whole of Sartrean literature of the truly free man, of 'l'Homme engagé'.

It follows that writing alone, however committed it may be to the encouragement of human liberty, can only be partially effective. Sartre seems to have acknowledged this fact eventually, as he confides to us in his autobiographical essay *Les Mots*:

> 11. Longtemps, j'ai pris ma plume pour une épée: à présent je connais notre impuissance. N'importe: je fais, je ferai des livres; il en faut; cela sert tout de même. La culture ne sauve rien ni personne, elle ne justifie pas. Mais c'est un produit de l'homme; il s'y projette, s'y reconnaît; seul, ce miroir critique lui offre, son image.
>
> (*Les Mots,* p. 211)

This book dates from 1963, but the disenchantment with literary work which it relates is obviously anterior to that date; Francis Jeanson situates the conversion quite definitely in 1954, and since Jeanson is a personal friend of Sartre, and his most respected critic, we may believe him. Sartre has avowed that his early work was the product of a 'neurosis', that (like Baudelaire) he had made writing an end in itself;

> 12. J'envisageai tranquillement que j'étais fait pour écrire. Par besoin de justifier mon existence, j'avais fait de la littérature un absolu. Il m'a fallu trente ans pour me défaire de cet état d'esprit. Quand mes relations avec le parti communiste m'ont donné le recul nécessaire, j'ai décidé d'écrire mon autobiographie. Je voulais montrer comment un homme peut passer de la littérature considérée comme sacrée à une action qui reste néanmoins celle d'un intellectuel.
>
> (Jean-Paul Sartre, in conversation with Jacqueline Piatier, quoted in Francis Jeanson's *Sartre par lui-même,* p. 116)

At best, Sartre seems to be saying, writing is an action which may justify the existence of the writer. Writing on social injustices in such a way as to provoke political upheavals is already an improvement, transcending, as it does, the concern with self to embrace the concern with all men. And Sartre has written millions of words on social and political matters. But, in the end, the only valid action which deserves the epithet 'engagé', which takes full account of man's responsibility to men, is direct political radicalism.

B. Political Action

In *Les Mains Sales*, Hoederer warns Hugo that it is not sufficient for him to support the aims of the Communist party on paper, he must be prepared to get his hands dirty, in other words, not to talk, but to *act*:

1. Comme tu tiens à ta pureté, mon petit gars! Comme tu as peur de te salir les mains. Eh bien, reste pur! A qui cela servira-t-il, et pourquoi viens-tu parmi nous? La pureté, c'est une idée de fakir et de moine. Vous autres, les intellectuels, les anarchistes bourgeois, vous en tirez prétexte pour ne rien faire. Ne rien faire, rester immobile, serrer les coudes contre le corps, porter des gants. Moi j'ai les mains sales. Jusqu'aux coudes. Je les ai plongées dans la merde et dans le sang.

Sartre moved out of the realm of 'pure' literature into 'committed' literature with the foundation of his political review *Les Temps Modernes* in 1945. Furthermore, most of his post-war plays are devoted to the discussion of some political problem or other. *Les Mains Sales* (1948) is concerned with the personal dilemma of an idealistic Communist. *La Putain Respectueuse* (1946) dealt with corrupt racialism in the United States of America. *Nekrassov* (1956) is a satire of the cold-war mentality very prevalent in the late forties. *Le Diable et le Bon Dieu* (1951) defends the use of violence in the pursuit of human progress. *Les Séquestrés d'Altona* (1959) discusses the problem of torture (allegations of torture by the French army in Algeria were rife in 1957–60, and were subsequently found to be justified).

Apart from a brief estrangement from the Soviets in 1956 (following the invasion of Hungary, which Sartre labelled inexcusable), Sartre has been a more or less vocal advocate in favour of Russia and the Communist state. He has never joined the Communist Party, and has been a vehement critic of the French Communist Party in particular. He certainly has no sympathy with the automatic card-carrying Communist who toes the party line without question. He portrayed one such character in *La Mort dans l'Ame*, Brunet, who takes refuge in the ready-made values of the Communist Party to avoid having to invent values of his own, or take any entirely authentic personal action.

Nor should it be assumed that Sartre subscribes to Marxist doctrine. There are many similarities between existentialism and Marxism, it is true, and Sartre has written much on the subject in his revue *Les Temps Modernes*; nevertheless, it must be obvious that Sartre's view of human reality stands in absolute opposition to the orthodox Marxist view, which regards man as an *object* in the stream of history. Sartrean existentialism, on the contrary, insists on the importance of individual human dignity and freedom.

For the same reason, Sartre is unlikely to be a partisan of the establishment of any particular ideology, of whatever colour or political inclination. The imposition of any specific political or social order would of necessity limit or shackle the individual human freedom to make personal choices, and this would be the greatest crime, commensurate with the imposition of a theological or moral code of values.

It is therefore misleading to suppose Sartre a Communist or a Marxist in the strictest sense. He does not recommend conformity to the dictated values of any 'ideal' society, but he does recommend social reform and protest against the abuses of the time, of the *situation*. His support for the Russian Communists derives from his belief that they are more likely than anyone to achieve social reform in the *situation* in which he finds himself; his political doctrine is better described as progressive socialism than as Communism, and as such, it is perfectly compatible with his philosophy.

Jean-Paul Sartre has not shrunk from getting his own 'hands dirty' in as much as he has always been ready to take a lead on political matters of French or international importance. He spoke out virulently against the French involvement in Algeria, has been a constant critic of American political morality, takes part in popular demonstrations at some considerable personal risk, travels all over the world to lend the weight of his authority to a myriad of causes, founded an anti-Fascist League in 1962, refused to accept the Nobel prize for Literature in 1964, sat on the Bertrand Russell War Crimes Tribunal in 1967, and has worked untiringly for the establishment of a better society.

Engagement has become for Sartre almost synonymous with an anti-bourgeois crusade, since he sees most of the social injustices which bedevil his fellow-men as deriving from bourgeois values and bourgeois 'rights'. Thus committed literature means for him literature committed to the betterment of the working classes.

In a way, it seems as if Sartre now rejects his early career as being the product, almost, of *mauvaise foi*. It is certainly true that the novels and early philosophic writings concentrated on demonstrating what freedom was without actually recommending any definite course of action by which to use this freedom. Sartre's position now is that the philosopher's task is to support the struggle of the working-classes against the bourgeoisie, against, in fact, the class from which he himself springs, even if the struggle should involve the use of violence.

Jean-Paul Sartre is, indeed, the best living example of *l'homme engagé*. So true has he remained to the principles which he has himself evolved (and which I have discussed in these pages), namely the responsibility of freedom and the necessity of action, that he has forsaken all literature which did no more than justify his own existence, and rescue himself from crushing absurdity, in order to concentrate all his efforts on the amelioration of the human condition. He has abandoned the analysis of the individual quest for freedom (*la Nausée, Les Chemins*) to concern himself with humanity in the mass. Sartre has made himself responsible (in his own eyes) for the justification of human existence. As Jeanson (himself a Marxist) has put it:

2. Il s'agissait de s'arracher seul au non-sens de sa propre contingence; il s'agit désormais de contribuer, parmi les hommes, à la seule entreprise qui les concerne tous et qui est de se rendre responsables de leur histoire.

(*Sartre par lui-même,* p. 183)

7
Conclusions

A. Humanist

There is no place in the Sartrean view of the world for theological discussion, no room for metaphysical discoveries, no need for the natural world in the Rousseauesque or Romantic tradition, no place for the animal kingdom. The only world which concerns Sartre is the human world. The only problems which merit discussion are human problems, the only conduct worth observing is human conduct. His vision is entirely anthropocentric. In this sense, Sartre is very much a humanist; he believes that human life is neither better nor worse than we make it. If it is good, there is no one we have to thank; if it is bad, there is no one we can blame. We are alone in the world, without excuses; we cannot fall back on any concept of a 'human nature' to explain why we are what we are; we *are* only what we *do*. And by our acts, we create and invent values.

Sartre is an atheist, but not one who would waste time discussing the merits or demerits of the existence of a deity. He simply dismisses God as an excuse which people use, in their *mauvaise foi*, for not doing anything. Having placed man at the centre of his universe, he does not consider God as a valid topic for consideration. The most he will allow is that it is perhaps a nuisance that God does not exist, but even if he did, it would not have much importance:

1. L'existentialisme n'est pas tellement un athéisme au sens où il s'épuiserait à démontrer que Dieu n'existe pas. Il déclare plutôt: même si Dieu existait, ça ne changerait rien; voilà notre point de vue. Non pas que nous croyions que Dieu existe, mais nous pensons que le problème n'est

pas celui de son existence; il faut que l'homme se retrouve lui-même et se persuade que rien ne peut le sauver de lui-même, fût-ce une preuve valable de l'existence de Dieu.

(*L'Existentialisme est un Humanisme*, p. 95)

Maurice Cranston has accused Sartre of putting the cart before the horse in claiming that man must invent his own values *because* God does not exist. Moral values are not derived from God anyway, says Cranston. They may be historically derived from some religious systems, but logically they are prior to a conception of the Deity, since the Deity is supposed to epitomize all that we consider to be 'good'; therefore, a concept of 'goodness' must precede a concept of a Being who possesses such virtue. But Sartre has made it quite clear that his contention we must create our own moral values is not made *on the grounds that* God does not exist, but *irrespective* of whether he exists or not. He only considers the existence of God because it is invoked by those with *mauvaise foi* as an explanation. He himself regards the matter as an irrelevance, belonging as it does to the realm of metaphysics (which deals in hypotheses) and not the realm of existence (which deals in facts).

Cranston does, however, make the interesting point that Sartre's existentialism belongs historically to religion. 'Sartre', he says, 'is an atheist who understands nothing better than Man's thirst for God, and whose lesson is that Man must learn to live with that thirst for ever unsatisfied.' It is interesting, also, that other existentialist philosophers are in fact Christian (Kierkegaard[1] and Gabriel Marcel,[2] for instance).

[1] *Soren Kierkegaard* (1813–1855). Commonly regarded as the founder of modern Existentialism, Kierkegaard was born in Copenhagen, where he became a distinguished theologian. His system was based on the antipathy between Thought and Existence. Among his works are *The Concept of Irony, Fear and Trembling, Repetition, The Concept of Anguish*.

[2] *Gabriel Marcel* Born in 1889, Marcel is both a philosopher and dramatist, converted to Catholicism in early middle-age. His first important work is *Journal Metaphysique* (1927).

F

Given that Man's search for God is fruitless, he must devote his energies to a search for himself, and to a search for Man. The Sartrean man displays a love for mankind in its deepest and most honest form, witnessed by what he does, not by what he thinks. Oreste addresses the crowd of Argos, after his double assassination, with the words: 'Et pourtant, ô mes hommes, je vous aime, et c'est pour vous que j'ai tué.' Sartre concludes his autobiography with the claim that his only worth is to be a man among men, 'un homme fait de tous les hommes et qui les vaut tous et que vaut n'importe qui.' (*Les Mots.*)

B. Optimist

Because it places such a stress on the *future*, Sartre's philosophy is also profoundly optimistic. He is full of hope that men can, and will, give meaning and dignity to their lives and control their own destiny:

1. L'homme est d'abord ce qui se jette vers un avenir, et ce qui est conscient de se projeter dans l'avenir.
   (*L'Existentialisme est un Humanisme,* p. 23)

2. Ponge a dit, dans un très bel article: 'l'homme est l'avenir de l'homme'. C'est parfaitement exact.   (Ibid, p. 38)

3. il n'y a pas de doctrine plus optimiste, puisque le destin de l'homme est en lui-même.   (Ibid, p. 62)

On the face of it, Sartre's teaching that life has no meaning until we give it one, may appear to be a counsel of despair. But his conviction that we *can* give life a meaning by our actions, and that we *can* make the future bright for humanity as a whole by accepting our engagement, makes the possible horrors of our present condition more endurable, by making them transient. Sartre's counsel is the voice of encouragement:

4. L'homme n'est point la somme de ce qu'il a, mais la totalité de ce qu'il n'a pas encore, de ce qu'il pourrait avoir. Et si nous baignons ainsi dans l'avenir, la brutalité informe du présent n'en est-elle pas atténuée?
   ('La temporalité chez Faulkner' in *Situations I,* p. 80)

To return once more to Baudelaire, it is easy to see why this man who finds his justification in his past, should be so antipathetic to Sartre. 'Il se défait plutôt qu'il n'évolue,' says Sartre (p. 208), and more precisely:

5. 'Baudelaire, qui ne *veut* rien entreprendre, tourne le dos à l'avenir.'   (p. 210)

It is also easy, in the light of the optimism inherent in Sartre's philosophy, to understand why *Huis-Clos* should be called a tragedy. Garcin, Inès and Estelle cannot possibly have a future, since they are already dead. This inability to act, to project oneself into a future, constitutes the most tragic situation imaginable. The three characters are doomed to remain as passive as a stone; they have no hope.

C. Morals

Sartre has frequently been accused of preaching amorality or, still worse, immorality. Gabriel Marcel, notably, a fellow philosopher and existentialist of the Christian variety, has written:

> Je n'hésite pas à dire, pesant mes mots, que dénigreur invétéré, blasphémateur systématique, il aura répandu autour de lui les enseignements les plus pernicieux, les conseils les plus toxiques qui aient jamais été prodigués à la jeunesse par un corrupteur patenté.
> (Gabriel Marcel, in *Les Nouvelles Littéraires*, 29 October 1964)

While it is true that the Sartrean idea of authentic action runs counter to the precepts of most established moral codes, it would be totally wrong to consider that this renders him an 'immoral' writer. On the contrary, Sartre's morality is at once more noble and more austere than orthodox morality:

– *noble*, because it says that men must act as the result of a difficult personal choice, and not as a simple obedience to written orders.

– *austere*, because, whatever they do, men must carry the burden of responsibility for their acts and their behaviour, and indeed, each man carries responsibility for the whole of mankind. Has there ever been a more rigorous morality than this?

What constitutes *immorality* for Sartre is blind adherence to past values, the refusal to take part in the drama of creating and defining man each day, the cowardly abnegation of life in favour of a comfortable, death-like being.

One may make the objection that absolute freedom and the inalienable right to individual personal choice might lead logically to anarchy. If each man is free to act as he deems fit, to invent his own values, what would happen if no two men were to act in the same way, and were to create values which differed from and conflicted with each other? What if a hundred men can invent a hundred different 'moralities'? Would not this promote utter chaos?

Such an objection leaves out of account the question of the *situation*, and the notion of *responsibility*.

The *situation* acts as a limiting factor, in so far as it must *per se* abridge the number of avenues open for action. Each man finds himself 'placed' in a certain group of circumstances, in a specific class of a specific society in a particular country at a particular point in history. Hippolyte Taine would have referred to 'la race, le milieu et le moment'. But whereas for Taine these factors are *deterministic*, for Sartre they are only *descriptive*.

One of the points of contention in Sartre's quarrel with Mauriac (to which I have referred in a previous chapter, dealing with the power of God over Mauriac's characters), is that Mauriac places too heavy an emphasis on the determining factors of the situation; that he regards the individual human being as an entity rigidly fashioned by circumstances, heredity, and environment. For Sartre, on the other hand, the situation acts as a frame within which and in relation to which man exercises his freedom; he insists that the situation can be changed or improved by the individual.

While therefore, the situation cannot determine an individual's behaviour, it does in a way *enclose* it, in the sense that any personal or social action must be taken in the context of that situation and be relevant to it if it is to be effective. Man is free, therefore, but he must take into account the situation in which he is free; to choose a course of action which is irrelevant to the situation would be to act irresponsibly, and one's act would be meaningless.

This brings me to the second answer to the objection of anarchy, which is the importance of *responsibility*. An anarchist wishes to overthrow the established order, but feels no compulsion to replace it with something better. Sartrean man wishes to overthrow the established order *so that* he may create a more meaningful life for himself and his fellows. In other words, a Sartrean existentialist would never act irresponsibly; his is a difficult and constructive task, subject to constant revision, the anarchist's is an easy and destructive task. Nevertheless, I think it fair to say that Sartre might prefer anarchy to apathy.

In the end, it is in the concept of *action* that Sartre's morality reveals all its severity. For he says, in effect, that a man *is* only what he *does,* and can be judged, if at all, only by his actions. Therefore, Sartre demands that we should be *honest, sincere,* and *true to our own values*, which we continue to create every day. It is a morality to which one cannot pay lip-service: it must be seen in one's deeds. One is constrained to 'practise what one preaches'.

8
Theory

It has been stressed in this essay that Sartre's philosophy is primarily an ethic of action, little concerned with the hair-splitting intricacies of philosophical theory. In a sense, it is anti-philosophical. It is none the less true that there is an ontological theory underlying the concept of freedom which forms the backbone of most of Sartre's fictional and critical work; this theory has been expounded in a number of philosophical works, but nowhere more exhaustively than in the long treatise *L'Être et le Néant*, published in 1943. The work is subtitled 'an essay on phenomenological ontology', which indicates that Sartre intends it to be a work of explanation, or description, rather than a system of hypothetical ideas on metaphysics. He wishes to elucidate what he considers to be the facts of existence as they are described in a more dramatic and assimilable fashion in his plays and novels.

The foundation of this theory is the distinction between, on the one hand, *consciousness*, and on the other, the *object* perceived by the consciousness. Consciousness cannot exist in a void, it must be consciousness *of something* exterior to itself. It only exists in so far as it is aware of exterior objects. One cannot therefore say 'I am conscious', but only 'I am conscious of that tree'. These separate but mutually necessary partners in the act of perception were defined by Heidegger as *Dasein* (the consciousness) and *Seiendes* (the objects of consciousness). Sartre makes his distinction between *L'En-soi* and le *Pour-soi*.

L'En-soi

L'En-soi is a term which designates what in *La Nausée* Sartre called more simply les Choses, the objects of consciousness. The *en-soi* is characterized by being invariable, unchangeable, incapable of movement. It simply *is*. This term would cover not only the root of the chestnut-tree (as in *La Nausée*), or this piece of paper before me, but also the person I was yesterday, the history of France, or the life of Benvenuto Cellini. *Things* such as these have no need of anything exterior in order to be. They are there, ugly, huge, amorphous, unassailable, insulting. Insulting, because I have no control over them, I cannot make them cease to be, or make them different from what they are. They form a chaos of unjustified beings, a maze of meaninglessness which is there as a sort of challenge. They are things 'in-themselves'.

Le Pour-soi

The consciousness which perceives the unremitting chaos of the en-soi is called *the Pour-soi*; it is characterized by the ability to change, to evolve, to question itself. Unlike the Things, whose description is determined, glued for ever in its past, present, and future state, the pour-soi represents ceaseless movement. One cannot say that consciousness 'is' in the same way that Things 'are'. It can never be a delimitable whole. I cannot therefore say that I 'am' a journalist, for example, only that I 'make myself' a journalist at the moment. Tomorrow I may make myself something different; yesterday has already become part of the *en-soi*. Similarly, my body is *en-soi*, but 'I' who contemplate it am *pour-soi*.

A more picturesque description of the *pour-soi* is given in Roquentin's diary:

> Moi. Le corps, ça vit tout seul, une fois que ça a commencé. Mais la pensée, c'est *moi* qui la continue, qui la déroule. J'existe. Je pense que j'existe. Oh, le long serpentin, ce sentiment d'exister. . . .

Ma pensée, c'est *moi*: voilà pourquoi je ne peux pas m'arrêter. J'existe par ce que je pense . . . et je ne peux pas m'empêcher de penser. En ce moment même – c'est affreux – si j'existe *c'est parce que* j'ai horreur d'exister. C'est moi, *c'est moi* qui me tire du néant auquel j'aspire: la haine, le dégoût d'exister, ce sont autant de manières de *me faire* exister, de m'enfoncer dans l'existence. Les pensées naissent par derrière moi comme un vertige, je les sens naître derrière ma tête . . . si je cède, elles vont venir là devant, entre mes yeux – et je cède toujours, la pensée grossit, grossit, et la voilà, l'immense, qui me remplit tout entier et renouvelle mon existence.

(*La Nausée*, pp. 142–3)

Le Néant

The function of consciousness (le *pour-soi*), is to observe Things (l'*en-soi*), clarify them, and give meaning to them. This it does by selection, by detaching an object from the mass of formless objects in order to endow it with shape and meaning. When I say, 'There is a table', my consciousness is distinguishing itself from that table and at the same time distinguishing the table from all other appearances which constitute the *en-soi*. It must therefore temporarily annihilate or nullify the rest of the *en-soi*, throw it meanwhile into a state of nothingness. This process Sartre calls *néantisation*. In other words, for the length of time that it takes for consciousness to perceive an object, give it shape and meaning, all other objects cease to exist, or rather remain in their amorphous state of 'being'; consciousness therefore, in selecting the table and distinguishing it from everything else, denies existence to everything else, which then becomes nothingness. Nothingness (*le néant*) comes into the world through consciousness, or through the action of the *pour-soi* on the *en-soi*. 'L'être considéré est *cela*, et en dehors de cela, *rien*.' (*L'Être et le Néant*, p. 43) or, to use Norman Greene's phrase, consciousness is nothingness 'because it is a translucent awareness of something it is not.'

Just as consciousness 'néantise' the vast mass of Things in

order to select one and give it meaning, so also it nullifies what it was itself yesterday, or last month, or last year. The past of the *pour-soi* is part of the *en-soi*, and thus is subject to *néantisation*. To return to the example 'I make myself a journalist', which signifies that I am perpetually creating myself, and am never fixed in a stagnant state of being like the Things: if I wish, I can tomorrow cease to make myself a journalist; I would reject the 'journalist-that-I-was' into a state of nothingness. In this way, man transcends himself, or, in other terms, consciousness always rejects with contempt that which it was. Man is continually re-creating himself; like Sisyphus, he can never be satisfied, never reach his goal, will always be frustrated. He can never achieve the stability of an *en-soi*.

One can recognize in the above sketch of the basics of Sartrean ontology all the concepts that we have found in dramatic form elsewhere.

1. En-soi =· les Choses = stagnation = passivity.
2. Pour-soi = consciousness == freedom = action. (Existence precedes Essence.)
3. Le Néant = ability to choose and give significance, to create Essences.

I have said elsewhere that Oreste, in *Les Mouches*, rejects the idea that he 'is' an avenger, in order to create his own justification for existence, to invent his own definition through the medium of free action. In ontological terms, one could now say that Oreste, as *pour-soi*, rejects the *en-soi* that he was by means of casting it into nothingness (*le Néant*), or by nullifying his own past self. What he was is *L'Être* (like a stone or a table), a state from which he will rescue himself by *le Néant*, the ability of his consciousness to choose, change, and move forward. In Francis Jeanson's words:

> L'orgueil Sartrien, ce sera ainsi le refus de soi en tant qu'être donné et l'exigence acharnée de se produire soi-même en se néantisant.　　(*Sartre par lui-même*, p. 149)

Être-pour-autrui

Up to this point, it might seem that Sartre's view of the world was entirely solipsistic, but this would be misleading. The individual consciousness does not consider itself the *only* real existant, the *only* giver of significance to the Things which surround it; it is also acutely aware of the existence of other consciousnesses, which are also instances of 'pour-soi', and which are also therefore free. I (as pour-soi) have awareness (a) of Things (l'en-soi), and (b) of other people (more 'pour-soi'). But two 'pour-soi' entities cannot meet without a collision, since each is free, and each will seek to use its freedom to interpret, define, delineate the Other, which, being free, will resist being interpreted, defined, delineated. Therefore, the freedom of the Other is incompatible with mine.

When I look at the Other, I transfix him in his present state; he becomes the thing-that-is-looked-at and ceases to be free. When he looks at me, similarly, I am captured in a Thing-like state of 'en-soi', and cease to be free. A harmonious social life becomes impossible under these conditions, and still more so, a happy relationship between two people. In a love-relationship, each partner, by virtue of the simple exercise of his or her consciousness, is destroying the freedom of the other partner; the moment the pour-soi operates (and it *cannot cease* to operate, or, in other words, we are condemned to be free), the object of its consciousness becomes, precisely, an object. Relationships between free people are inevitably based on *conflict*. In my relationship with the loved one, the only way in which I can resolve the conflict is for my freedom to be victorious and for his or her freedom to succumb and allow itself to be enslaved. This is another way of saying that human relationships are based on power, and are successful only on a sado-masochistic level. If my freedom wins, I am being sadistic, and the Other is being masochistic.

Sartre finds more evidence for masochism in human relationships than for sadism. He says that the desperate desire of men to mean something, to have an essence, to possess the passive tranquillity of a Thing, leads them masochistically to renounce their freedom and allow the Other to solidify them, to petrify them. It works like this: I am terrified of the loneliness of the 'pour-soi', of the terrible necessity to create myself all the time. Freedom *is* not anything, it makes other things *be*; so if I continue to exercise my freedom, I can never myself *be* anything; the only way I can *be* anything, carry within myself the dignity of a fixed significance or essence, is to allow myself to be petrified in the gaze of another, to become a Thing. I cannot *mean* anything except in his eyes; I therefore succumb, he dominates me, and my 'pour-soi' becomes 'en-soi'. I am now happy.

It is clear that all the relationships in Sartrean literature reflect this view of sado-masochistic struggle. No two people ever achieve a harmonious relationship with each retaining his freedom and the respect of the other; by the very nature of Sartre's view of human intercourse, such a relationship is impossible. Daniel, in *Les Chemins de la Liberté*, is the best example of the man who attempts to achieve tranquillity through masochism: he yields himself up to the power of the Others; he will *be* the homosexual that they see him to be; he will no longer have to worry about creating his own essence, it has been created for him. In ontological language, Daniel has allowed his pour-soi to become en-soi. Mathieu accuses him of self-martyrdrom (*L'Age de Raison*, p. 436).

In the pages of *L'Être et le Néant*, Sartre presents a depressing catalogue of other futile attempts at human relationships which are all basically variations on the theme of sado-masochism. He states quite categorically that they are all doomed to failure because it is impossible for two consciousnesses to confront each other without one of them ceasing to be consciousness; each will try to transcend the other and neither can be transcended while still remaining consciousness.

Mauvaise Foi

The *pour-soi* yearns for the stability of the *en-soi* and would like of achieve such stability but still retain, at the same time, its freedom. It aspires to be an *en-soi-pour-soi*, an impossible goal since it is a contradiction in terms. If such a being were possible, he would be God, i.e. the being who creates essences and is at the same time the possessor of the sum of all those essences, or the being who is what he wants to be.

Only despair can result from such an effort. Sartre has said that man is fundamentally the desire to be God, but his message is that this desire is unrealizable and that one must accept the despair which results from it. Only when the despair has been accepted, can the authentic, constructive life begin. As Oreste says in *Les Mouches*:

> la vie humaine commence de l'autre côté du désespoir.

It does however require a resolute effort beyond the capacity or willingness of many people to accept the despair which Sartre says is inevitable; in the face of their inability to be an *en-soi-pour-soi*, many men will take the easiest way out, which is to make themselves simply an *en-soi*. In other words, if they cannot have stability *and* freedom, they would prefer to have stability alone.

This is a desire which can only be attained by what Sartre has called *la mauvaise foi*.

In a previous chapter, I have discussed the various ways in which bad faith manifests itself in the lives of men who attempt to mask their freedom. It is sufficient here to say that there is no answer to bad faith in Sartrean ontology.

If I should disagree with Sartre's view of the world, and claim that I have found it possible to achieve a relationship with another person which does not negate the freedom of either of us, I should be guilty of bad faith. If, again, I should decide that I choose, in my freedom, to renounce that freedom because I want to, I should also be guilty of bad faith. I may decide that

I prefer a relationship based on masochism to no relationship at all, but my decision would be taken in bad faith. For Sartre, bad faith is as much a *fact* in his ontology as are consciousness, the objects of consciousness, freedom and responsibility. Although I am free at all times to choose whatever meaning I wish for myself, I am not free to choose *not* to choose.

A useful synopsis of the various constituent parts of Sartrean ontology is given in Professor Greene's book:

> In summary, reality as Sartre pictures it is composed of objects and subjects, being-in-itself and being-for-itself. The category of objects includes the surrounding material world, but also any other object of consciousness, including the individual self as seen in introspection and individual behaviour as seen by others, or being-for-others. The subject is consciousness, which is not essentially thinking or deliberation but rather awareness, in the sense that one can be aware or conscious of deliberating. That which exists is not subjectivity as such, but various individual instances of subjectivity. In each instance of subjectivity we find not a new kind of being, but a process by which being becomes aware of itself.
>
> (Norman N. Greene, *Jean-Paul Sartre*; p. 21)

At one point in his career, Sartre seemed about to suggest that a relationship between two people was after all possible. In his review *Les Temps Modernes* in 1949 he published the first two chapters of Volume IV of *Les Chemins de la Liberté*, entitled *Une Drôle d'Amitié*. He described the beginnings of a love relationship between Brunet and Vicarios, which was based neither on masochism nor on sadism, and which appeared to be successful. But the relationship was never developed, and the book was never finished. Since that time, Sartre has abandoned his study of individual relationships, which he now regards as fruitless, and concentrated more and more on the only relationship which does not compromise individual freedom, and that is the relationship of the individual to mankind as a whole. The only action which maintains the autonomy of the *pour-soi* and creates meaning in the world which does not entail the chaining of another *pour-soi*, is social commitment. The salvation of the individual lies in his conscious work towards the progress of mankind, towards a better life for his fellows.

Sartre's main purpose is to remind us that we all share the responsibility for giving meaning and dignity to human life in general. It is not enough that we should pay lip-service to one ideology or another, one political system or another, or that we should espouse the cause of a theory. He tells us that human life will only have value if each and every one of us strives actively to invest it with a value. His message is a salutary one. Maurice Cranston has described Sartre's aim in the following terms:

> He is a stern moralist who teaches above all things the need to be responsible and mature. He believes that virtue is possible, but difficult; that the world can be changed for the better, but that change demands a resolute effort.
> (Maurice Cranston, *Sartre*, p. 11)

Bibliography

A. Chronological list of works by Jean-Paul Sartre

L'Imagination, Paris (Presses Universitaires de France), 1936

La Nausée, Paris (Gallimard), 1938

Le Mur, Paris (Gallimard), 1939

Esquisse d'une théorie des Émotions, Paris (Hermann), 1939

L'Imaginaire: psychologie phénoménologique de l'imagination, Paris (Gallimard), 1940

Les Mouches, Paris (Gallimard), 1943

L'Être et le Néant, essai d'ontologie phénoménologique, Paris (Gallimard), 1943

L'Age de Raison, Paris (Gallimard), 1945

Le Sursis, Paris (Gallimard), 1945

Huis-Clos, Paris (Gallimard), 1945

L'Existentialisme est un Humanisme, Paris (Nagel), 1946

La Putain Respectueuse, Paris (Nagel), 1946

Réflexions sur la Question Juive, Paris (Morihien), 1946

Baudelaire, Paris (Gallimard), 1947

Situations I, Paris (Gallimard), 1947

Théâtre (including *Les Mouches, Huis-Clos, Morts sans Sépultures,* and *La Putain Respectueuse*), Paris (Gallimard), 1947.

Les Jeux sont faits, Paris (Nagel), 1947

L'Engrenage, Paris (Nagel), 1948

Les Mains Sales, Paris (Gallimard), 1948

Situations II (including *Qu'est-ce que la Littérature?*) Paris (Gallimard), 1948

La Mort dans L'Ame, Paris (Gallimard), 1949

Situations III, Paris (Gallimard), 1949

Entretiens sur la Politique (with David Rousset & Gérard Rosenthal), Paris (Gallimard), 1949